A Modern Ninety-Five

A Modern Ninety-Five

Questions Today's Evangelicals Need to Answer

Nancy A. Almodovar

RESOURCE Publications · Eugene, Oregon

A MODERN NINETY-FIVE
Questions Today's Evangelicals Need to Answer

Copyright © 2008 Nancy A. Almodovar. All rights reserved. Except for brief quotations in critical publications or reviews, no part of this book may be reproduced in any manner without prior written permission from the publisher. Write: Permissions, Wipf and Stock, 199 W. 8th Ave., Suite 3, Eugene, OR 97401.

www.wipfandstock.com

ISBN 13: 978-1-55635-678-0

Manufactured in the U.S.A.

For my loving husband, Roberto

Contents

Acknowledgments ix

Foreword xi

Introduction xiii

1. Apostles/Prophets 1
2. Can We Know Absolute Truth? 21
3. Oops, They Did It Again! 39
4. Two Classes of Christians 70
5. Down They Go ... Again! 81
6. Just a Little Discernment, Please! 90
7. Protestant Indulgences with Prophets and Profiteers 99
8. Another Gospel: "You Too Can Be Gods" and Other Assorted Heresies 112
9. Doctrine Matters: The True Gospel 124
10. Seeking Purposes or Trusting Sovereign Promises? 145
11. The Final Word 161

Bibliography 171

Acknowledgments

It would be impossible for me to acknowledge all those who have contributed to the completion of this book. This project has been in the works for over three years and during that time there were those providentially sent to me and I to them who challenged the validity and veracity of questions such as those posed in this book. These are the ones who I would like to personally thank at this time.

First, I want to thank my husband, Rev. Roberto Almodovar, who has since the day we met challenged me to accomplish tasks I thought impossible. Over three years ago, when I began to see that much of what I had been taught in church was at best wrong and at worst heretical, he challenged me to ask the tough questions. However, he would not leave me at just asking but would confront me to bring those questions to the scriptures and see how the Bible actually answers them. As the project began to develop, it was my ever-faithful husband who began to see that my questions were becoming numerous and jokingly asked if I was putting together another Ninety-five Theses in the vein of Martin Luther's. As question piled upon question, soon there were ninety-five and the premise of this book was born. For the next three years he would ask, "Is the book done yet?" Through his gentle guidance and encouragement, this book now stands complete. Thank you, Bobby, for encouraging and equipping me to fight the good fight of faith and contend for the truth handed down to us.

Next, there are several who read this book as it was developing and helped in content and in maintaining its faithfulness to the scriptures. Those are D. Philip Veitch, a retired navy chaplain who would direct me to "fire for effect" in order to confront the pulpit and yet care for the pew. His encouragement to battle the errors and call them out has strengthened my resolve to speak out against these errors. Thanks to David Genna, who graciously wrote the foreword of this book and has survived the same church waters I once swam. Special thanks to Dr. Gus Gianello who reviewed the manuscript for content as well as its biblical and theological sustenance, graciously adding to this book the wisdom of those who have

Acknowledgments

battled hard and often, have been wounded, and desire to warn other warriors to maintain battle stations on the frontline of truth.

To my dear friend, Mindy Rice, who patiently went through each chapter line by line correcting spelling, grammar, and continuity. Her encouragement to reveal my own fall into error gave this book its personal touch and testimony both to the failure of believers testing what they are taught as well as to the gracious mercy of our Lord who will not leave his elect in error for long.

To the board of directors of Silent Cry Ministries—my husband, Rev. Roberto Almodovar, the Rev. James Erle, Mrs. Jean Erle, and David Genna—thank you for following scripture as we became more aware of the errors we had fallen into. Thank you for moving toward the historical, redemptive, and Christological view of scripture along with us and for remaining faithful to God's word even when it meant we had taught wrongly in the past. Your support and encouragement, challenges and debates helped sharpen the skills this apologist needs.

To the church in our home, Tulip Reformed Church, for graciously pitching in to help with the weekly duties while I finished the manuscript and encouraging me through your faithfulness to God's word and his Son Jesus Christ. Your hunger for the truth and stalwart opposition to error has shown me that God maintains and preserves his remnant.

I wish to thank you, the reader, for picking up this book. If you are lost within any of the movements discussed in these pages, it is my prayer that God will reveal to you his truth through his word. If these professional hucksters have never trapped you, I pray that you will become more compassionate for those still held by the dark chains of purchasing God's favor or any other various errors. There are those within these movements who are truly of the elect of God, so tenderly reach out to them and lead them to the green pastures of truth. But should you come into contact with any promoting these lies and heresies, I pray you will not falter but contend for the truth passed down to you.

Finally, I must thank my Lord and Savior Jesus Christ, whose righteousness is now mine, whose obedience my obedience, and whose resurrection is my justification. Had God not saved me and kept me even during the years spent aimlessly within the Charismatic/Word of Faith and Prophetic/Apostolic movements, I might still be wallowing in that muck and mire. It is his gracious love that brought me out of darkness into his glorious light.

Foreword

THIS BOOK IS FOR all who seek the truth. Paul tells us that if even an angel of light were to preach a different "good news" than is written in the Bible, we are *not* to believe it. The words of our teachers and preachers should constantly be checked against the word of truth. This is a tall order, since the Bible was written in other languages using cultural references of a world changed by the passage of thousands of years.

So how do we find biblical truth? Many Christians are dependant on their pastors to interpret the word for modern life. Just because someone has Bishop, Apostle, Pastor, or Reverend in front of their name does not mean that he or she speaks for God. Unfortunately, all teachers and preachers are human, with unconscious needs and desires that color their interpretations. Tragically, some are even false prophets, out to line their pockets at the expense of the faithful. How can Christians protect themselves from wolves while seeking to deepen their faith?

To hear lies being perpetrated in the name of God and not to speak out against them is to commit the sin of silence. In this book, Nancy Almodovar exposes some of the most pernicious lies of our time. I have had the privilege of knowing Nancy along most of her journey. Her search for truth led her to study under many different ministers, in different denominations, and then to see that most of us have some kernel of truth. She learned that the most important thing is to test, ask questions, and compare everything to the word.

This book will challenge believers to ask those tough questions. It will challenge us to not simply say amen to every statement, but to search for the biblical foundations of truth and to expose false doctrines and ideas of men that have crept into the church in the guise of "new revelations." It will help us to hear God's voice through the din of conflicting doctrines. I trust that this book will help you "rightfully divide the Word of truth" (2 Tim 2:15).

—David Genna

Introduction

In the words of Martin Luther, "Out of love for the truth and the desire to bring it to light,"[1] the following propositions need to be discussed in their entirety by church leaders, pastors, and laymen alike. The Church is in danger of numerous heresies and various errors that have not been dealt with except on occasion by individuals. Therefore it is duly noted that the Church should come to a national discussion and debate of the various teachings that have arisen over the centuries since the Reformation that have caused many to fall into error.

—Humbly submitted by Nancy A. Almodovar

Over the past twenty years, my Christian life has been guided by the various teachings that I will discuss in this thesis. When Christ converted me in September 1986, I had a keen awareness that God was sovereign. However, as I sat under different ministers and their teachings, much of what the Bible actually teaches was clouded by pragmatism, Charismata, and the ideas of men. Instead of sitting under exegetical preaching (the type of preaching that seeks to understand what the text means or communicates on its own) I was constantly fed eisegetical teaching (teaching that sought to read into the text the preacher or teacher's own ideas) above the continuity of the whole Scripture.

Far from desiring to be critical in this endeavor, my heartfelt cry is that those who have walked down the paths that I have traveled will come to find, as I did, how *repulsive* many of these modern teachings are. There is no one who is immune to the errors that pervade evangelical Christianity today. Unless we are, as Peter said to be, "prepared to make a defense to anyone who asks you for a reason for the hope that is in you" (1 Pet 3:15), even other believers can be deceived. Jesus warned us that if it were possible in the last days "the elect" would be deceived (Mark 13:22).

---

1. Nichols, *Martin Luther's Ninety-five Theses*.

Introduction

This is a scary thought for those who value scripture and desire only the truth.

Oftentimes I have come across believers who are sincere in their pursuits of the "anointing" because they believe that it is needed to understand God better, know the scriptures more, and live a more victorious life. John in his letter to the churches warned the believers of those who would say they needed something additional in order to understand God better. He taught us, by the Holy Spirit, that we already have this "anointing" and already understand what is necessary for salvation (cf. 1 John 2:27). I do not fault the believers themselves, because this is what they have been taught. Instead, I condemn the teachers and preachers who have been deficient in their study of Scriptures by taking experiences and placing them above the *final authority of the written Word*. The pulpits are where the problems lie, and it has flooded down to the pews and crippled God's people with the cancer of heresy and deception (cf. Jude 1:3).

Therefore, this book has a two-fold purpose. First, it is a warning to the leaders of today's churches to bend their knees once again to what the scriptures teach and submit under the lordship of Jesus Christ and teach the faith once handed down to them. Second, it is an alarm to the people in the pews to run from the false teachers who would use them to build their ivory palaces with their "seed money" and spew false teachings (or nonsense) across the television screens, over the radio waves, and across the Internet in the guise of "prophetic utterances." This is a clarion call to return to the truth because "The truth will set you free" (John 8:32).

As I said earlier, *no one* is immune to these errors and heresies. I count myself in that group. Moving from Pentecostalism, semi-Pelagianismand Arminianism, through to the Charismatic movement, along the byways of the prophetic and apostolic movements, and into the darkness of deliverance ministries, I wandered for over fifteen years. I ran after the newest teachings thinking that they were true but instead found myself swallowed in the mire of error and the muck of heresy.

It is from deep concern over what is going on in modern Christianity because of the popular teachings publicized across the world that this book is written. The teachings of pastors and teachers trouble me with their special "revelations." Special "prophets" and "apostles" today receive and preach on TV, preach over the radio, and put into their books heresies that frighten me and cause me to think that we may be heading into

Introduction

another dark age. My heart is heavy because we have been bewitched and seduced by those who look like sheep but are in actuality wolves.

I too was caught in the thrill of hearing a word from the Lord, of being "slain" in the spirit, of prophesying over others, including many sincere and eager believers. Caught up in the excitement and ecstasy of the "anointing," I forgot that all we need for life and godliness has already been provided for (cf. 1 Pet 1:3). We seek words of knowledge and wisdom when God has provided both sufficiently in his written word and in the word of God incarnate, Jesus Christ (cf. Col 3:16). I am also very aware of the grave error that I taught. Trapped in the thrill, I let my guard down, did not check out what I was being taught against the scriptures, and helped to disperse these errors and heresies. However, the grace of God has shown me the beauty of his law and his word and it is this transcendent splendor that I want to bring to the forefront again. With the help of God, I will endeavor to bring the truth—truth that can be examined in the scriptures and validated by God's word. I offer to you, the reader, the gospel of God, knowing that his purpose will be performed even though I am woefully inadequate for the job.

A dear friend of mine, Mindy Rice, who helped edit this book, suggested that I share some of my personal experiences within the Word of Faith and Prophetic movements. I do not despise these people. It is not that I am disillusioned but rather that I was innocent, naïve, and trusting—like so many today. It is important to know that even if you have been corrupted by these destructive heresies, God's mercy extends as far as the east is from the west (Ps 103:12).

In March 2004, I received a phone call from a "prophetess." This was her "word from the Lord" for me:

> You will be taken to a city of habitation where your faith will be renewed. In that city of habitation multitudes of broken hearts and bleeding hearts will find healing. Go! And be Christ's ambassadors. He is sending you to a place you've never been before. This is the year of the Lord. You will go and speak the word in power and in the anointing. He is taking you to a higher place of authority. God has given you and your husband a place where only you can go—a place where only you fit. I see opening doors. Walk through them. Do not fear! I'm opening them. You are going to move stronger in the prophetic; My Spirit will go with you. Situations may seem impossible with man, but all things are possible with God. Do not look at the natural. I am bringing forth that which I planted in you

Introduction

> long ago. You are to step into the water and it will part before you. Something dangerous is coming in your life. Do not look at the storm but praise me and I'll see you through in a place of restoration of your soul and renewing and refreshing. I have a mighty work for you to do. Do not look to the storms when they come. They will challenge you. Look to me always. People in the body will challenge you, but they will not touch you. The danger will not strike you. Be a soldier. "Put on the whole armor." The time is short, Nancy. Do not let man hold you back. Do not listen to those who talk sweet. They will try to harm you. Do not receive any negative words. Say you will only listen to the Spirit of God and shake off their negative words. You have a strong prophetic gift. You move powerfully in the prophetic. You will be even stronger. I am going to answer prayers you haven't even thought to ask. I am going to supply things you haven't asked for yet! Spend time with me.

It was all well intended, yet almost every point was dead wrong. Nothing "harmed me." No one "came against me." Prayers "I did not ask" were not answered. At least it is impossible to know whether or not they were, since I did not ask them. Nor were my husband and I "sent to a place only we could go." None of the above came to pass.

From one of our own newsletters, you can see that the gospel message we proclaimed was not in line with Scripture. Please take note of the line at the end in italics.

> But first, we want to thank the women of "New Dawn Ministries" in Brooklyn for their warmth and hospitality and of course, their delicious meal at our last Princess Day. We are still hearing reports from the women who attended as to how God has healed them, restored them, brought them into a more intimate form of worship, and spoken to their personal needs through our staff.
>
> Nancy shared a message entitled "No Greater Love." Hearts were touched and many came forward afterwards for prayer. The most thrilling moment was when the sister of one of the attendees came forward at the altar call to commit her life to Jesus for the very first time. She shared with Nancy, "I never heard that God loved me so much. I want his love in my life." After Nancy prayed with her, the staff then counselled her, giving her a free Bible and other literature to help her in her walk with Jesus. *As Nancy prayed, many fell under the power of the Spirit and others were given prophetic words, as the Spirit led.*[2]

---

2. Almodovar, "Princess Day Update," 1.

Introduction

I am not angry with any of these teachers, because I am convinced that they are as deceived as I was. However still, many who know that what they are teaching is indeed a false gospel continue to teach this. Knowing that the Bible is the final and only authority, we as believers have the responsibility to warn others of their dangers and of the scarring it has caused so many. The questions I am posing in this book are questions that have come up over years of studying scriptures, reading historical Christian books, and learning from the two thousand years of biblical wisdom that is found in so many Christian movements that hold to "Sola Scriptura" (scripture alone). Much of what I have discovered is that today's Christianity is falling for the very teachings that historic Christianity labeled as error at best and heresy at worst.

Let me interject here with the saying, *"Those who refuse to learn from history will be condemned to repeat it."*[3] Why do we, when it comes to the political or military history, seek to find out what worked and what did not—what led to freedom and what brought bondage with such certainty? Yet when it comes to the history of the Church, the Body of Christ, true believers, we *shun the past* as if they were stuck in some *"dead religion."* Did true believers only show up again when Azusa Street occurred? Were there no real believers, born again and filled with the Spirit, between the late nineteenth century and the apostles' time? To think this is to completely misunderstand and underestimate God's power for his people in *every generation*. What we look at and label as *"dead orthodoxy"* is vital and vibrant faith in the Sovereign Lord who sits upon his throne and does whatsoever he pleases (Ps 115).

Somehow we have come to the conclusion that we are the only generation that is really saved. What pride! What arrogance! That we think we are better than the previous generations is pure haughtiness and conceit. The one thing that makes us so different than previous generations is that we have accepted teachings and doctrines that have been renounced and refuted by godly and wise believers in the past who God set within his Church to help keep their own and future generations from error. We have become so misled that we do not think we need their wisdom. We have fallen into almost every error, within one generation, that were usually present throughout the span of many generations.

---

3. Unknown Author, "Favorite PASTimes: Why Do History—and Historical Fiction—Matter?" Quote from Edmund Burke.

Introduction

We preach "discernment" from the *pulpits* but *neglect* to exercise it from the *pew* and find ourselves falling for Gnosticism in its newest incarnation: the teaching of "the anointing." We have failed to study the lives of our brothers and sisters who shed their blood for the purity of the gospel and balk at trials, "rebuking" them in the "name of Jesus" as if they could only be from the devil. It is these various errors and heresies that I wish to expose and uncover so that no one else falls into the pits that have been dug by charlatans, soothsayers, fortunetellers, and false prophets and anointed messengers.

Though I have endeavored to write out each scripture reference for ease of reading, it is highly recommended that you have your Bible with you while reading this book. The references and cross-references will be of high importance, enabling the reader to grasp the full content of scriptural portions.

It is my prayer and the cry of my heart that God will use this to awaken others, even to see the dangerous teachings (doctrines) that have been and continue to be foisted upon the Church since the end of the nineteenth century through to the twenty-first. I ask only that you prayerfully consider these pages and seek to compare today's teachings with what is written in the infallible word of God that we call scripture.

> If seduction and darkness were again to begin . . . and the devil were to begin to perform signs through some false prophet and perhaps cure a sick person, you would no doubt see the mob press to espouse the cause in such a way that no preaching or warning would be of any avail . . . For in those who have no love for the truth, the devil will be powerful and strong . . . If, then, these teachings (of a false prophet) contradict the chief doctrine and article of Christ, we should accord them neither attention or acceptance though it were to snow miracles daily.[4]

---

4. Plass and comp, *What Luther Says, An Anthology*, 637.

1

Apostles/Prophets

1. If the Church is built upon the foundation of the prophets and apostles, why is the foundation being laid a second time?

2. If there is a new foundation, what happened to the old foundation? Was it faulty or in need of repair? Was it removed?

3. If the so-called new apostles have met the Risen Christ, where did they see him?

4. And if they have seen him, should we not take heed to what our Lord said regarding visions of the Christ after his departure?

5. If the least of all apostles was St. Paul, the least being also the last, how is it that there are new apostles?

6. If Paul was not the last of the apostles, then scripture is in error.

7. If scripture is in error in this part, how are we to be assured of its accuracy in others?

8. The preaching that God is once again raising up prophets and apostles is laying again a foundation where one has already been laid.

9. We are taught, then, to fear our spiritual leaders and serve them, which is in exact opposition to our Lord's teachings that those who are greatest in the Kingdom are to be servants of all.

10. This is utter pride as even King David, the greatest of the anointed kings, was confronted by a servant of the Lord in his sin. He was called to account for his iniquities and judgment was proclaimed upon himself and his family.

11. *These influential men encourage us to rejoin Rome, hugging the harlot. They encourage us to discard the fact that Rome is diametrically opposed to the biblical doctrine of justification by faith and instead embrace them as brothers and sisters for the sake of unity. Compromise is the cancer that kills churches.*

12. *Seated in their ivory palace in Kansas City, these modern-day apostles and prophets would place the chain of imprisonment upon our necks and lead us back to Rome and slavery with their doctrine of ecumenicalism and universalism, trapping us again in the harlotry of that wicked and evil antichrist, the pope, and committing whoredom with the kingdoms of this world.*

These statements begin where the greatest error lies: taking authority that no longer belongs to us—that of apostle and prophet.

The basic aspect of all these statements is to understand the terms that have been employed by the Church Militant compared with the modern idea used by Pentecostals and Charismatics. If we fail to learn from previous generations of how this term "apostle" was interpreted by Bible-believing Christians, then we will fall into the same errors generation after generation. In history it is said that if someone has not learned from it, he or she is doomed to repeat it. We must line up our interpretations with those of other Christian leaders who have honored scripture in times past in order to continue our faithful exegesis of God's word.

Therefore, if by the term "apostle" we mean "one who is sent on a mission,"[1] then that is still a functioning office. If by the term we mean one who has biblical authority, has seen the Risen Christ personally, has infallibility in preaching, has a direct call from God, and performs signs and wonders on demand, then this is the criteria by which we challenge the claimant to prove by the written word of God that his or her authority is from above.

If by prophet we mean one who speaks the *revealed word of God* or as Merriam Webster's Collegiate Dictionary says, "An effective or leading spokesman for a cause, doctrine, or group," I have no quarrel with this preacher. If, however, we speak of a prophet as one who speaks "words" from God that have not been revealed in scripture, or who speaks foretelling events and is not 100 percent accurate 100 percent of the time, this

---

1. In *Merriam Webster Collegiate Dictionary*, http://www.m-w.com/dictionary/apostle (accessed August 22, 2007).

is a charlatan who must be challenged to show by what spirit he or she speaks.

Again, these statements/questions are posited to the leaders in their Plexiglas pulpits and from their TV stations to answer for their abuses, errors, heresies, and anti-biblical teachings. For the pew Christian, true discernment is needed so he may act as the noble Bereans to test and see if indeed it is the wheat of the word of God or the poisonous tares (weeds) of the word of man.

> It was the characterizing peculiarity of specifically the Apostolic Church, and it belonged therefore exclusively to the Apostolic age—although no doubt this designation may be taken with some latitude. These gifts were not the possession of the primitive Christian as such, nor for that matter of the Apostolic church or the Apostolic age for themselves; they were distinctively the authentication of the apostles. They were part of the credentials of the apostles as the authoritative agents of God in founding the Church. Their function thus confined them to distinctively the Apostolic Church, and they necessarily passed away with it.[2]

Yet, the claims that modern-day apostles and prophets make is that God is once again restoring these foundation offices to prepare the world for the second coming of Christ.

> And the Lord says, "*I'm giving you new grace* to begin to operate and function apostolically and prophetically like you've never known before and there is a new dimension of my grace and my glory that's even being released upon my leaders in this hour and you shall rise up with a new force and with a new authority and with a new power and with a new strength and with a new dynamic in your churches and you shall begin to see breakthroughs that you've never seen before," says the Lord. "For I break off the limitations that have tried to hold you back and have tried to hold back your gift and have tried to hold back your church, I begin to break the limitations through apostolic and prophetic release," *so the Lord said. "Get ready, I'm shifting you, I'm moving you into a new grace.* For all over the earth there is a new breed being raised up. There was a new leadership coming into place and many men and women are taking their place in leadership and *the apostles are rising and the prophets are rising and even the elders of the local*

---

2. Warfield. *Counterfeit Miracles*, 5–6.

churches are rising into a new dimension of grace to begin to release that which is not been released in generations."[3]

In scripture there is no mention of successors to Peter or the apostles except the place that was vacated by the traitor Judas Iscariot. However, Peter in his discourse in the upper room gives the criteria for apostleship which we read in Acts 1:21-22.

> So one of the men who have accompanied us during all the time that the Lord Jesus went in and out among us, beginning from the baptism of John until the day when he was taken up from us—one of these men must become with us a witness to his resurrection. (Acts 1:21-22)

The position of the apostles was unique to them and to Paul—all directly chosen by Christ Jesus with no hint of succession. In the New Testament, the apostles appointed not apostles but rather elders and deacons. This false presupposition is the essence of the papacy and all other churches that believe in "apostolic succession." It is a huge system based on the concept of apostolic succession. *Apostolic succession is a fraud and it is no accident of history that the Charismatic movement has found its strongest ally in the papal church.* The Lord God never entrusted his truth to a personal succession of any body of men. Such a foundation is flawed. Visible apostolic succession throughout history is impossible—it is impossible for popes and modern-day apostles and prophets. There is no sacramental ordination of one apostle by another, which is the key concept of the whole satanic doctrine.

What were the criteria for apostleship? Let's look at Acts 1:15-26.

> In those days Peter stood up among the brothers (the company of persons was in all about 120) and said, "Brothers, the scripture had to be fulfilled, which the Holy Spirit spoke beforehand by the mouth of David concerning Judas, who became a guide to those who arrested Jesus. For he was numbered among us and was allotted his share in this ministry." (Now this man acquired a field with the reward of his wickedness, and falling headlong he burst open in the middle and all his bowels gushed out. And it became known to all the inhabitants of Jerusalem, so that the field was called in their own language Akeldama, that is, Field of Blood.) "For it is written in the Book of Psalms, 'May his camp become desolate, and let there be no one to dwell in it'; and 'Let another take his office.'

---

3. Eckhardt, "Mobilizing the Prophetic Office."

Apostles/Prophets

> So one of the men who have accompanied us during all the time that the Lord Jesus went in and out among us, beginning from the baptism of John until the day when he was taken up from us—one of these men must become with us a witness to his resurrection." And they put forward two, Joseph called Barsabbas, who was also called Justus, and Matthias. And they prayed and said, "You, Lord, who know the hearts of all, show which one of these two you have chosen to take the place in this ministry and apostleship from which Judas turned aside to go to his own place." And they cast lots for them, and the lot fell on Matthias, and he was numbered with the eleven apostles.

But here we read Peter giving the criteria. To be an apostle, you had to have been with Jesus during his entire three years of ministry. You must have been called to follow from the beginning or as Peter says, "From the Baptism of John." In other words, you must have been there, in that particular place, at that particular time. You also had to have seen the physically risen Savior, as Paul did on the road to Damascus, and have been personally taught by Jesus, as we learn from Paul's letter to the Galatians that he had been (cf. Gal 1:1, 12).

Now these qualifications alone should make us recognize that there is no one today who can rightly fulfill these qualifications. One may argue that one was baptized and therefore follows Christ from his or her baptism onward, thereby enabling him or her to be an apostle, but this is *horrible* exegesis (explanation of text). You must have been there at the time Jesus physically walked the dusty roads of Judah during the time of the Roman occupation. If you were not there, physically there, then you cannot be an apostle in the New Testament sense of the word.

Objections may arise about Paul. He was not a follower of Christ while Jesus was in the flesh. However, we have already shown that each apostle was called and were chosen specifically and called by Jesus himself and that without a personal call to this office, you have no right to take it upon yourself.

Here is the account from Acts on Paul's conversion and appointment to the office of apostle:

> Now as he went on his way, he approached Damascus, and suddenly a light from heaven flashed around him. And falling to the ground he heard a voice saying to him, "Saul, Saul, why are you persecuting me?" And he said, "Who are you, Lord?" And he said, "I am Jesus, whom you are persecuting. But rise and enter the

city, and you will be told what you are to do." The men who were travelling with him stood speechless, hearing the voice but seeing no one. Saul rose from the ground, and although his eyes were opened, he saw nothing. So they led him by the hand and brought him into Damascus. And for three days he was without sight, and neither ate nor drank. Now there was a disciple at Damascus named Ananias. The Lord said to him in a vision, "Ananias." And he said, "Here I am, Lord." And the Lord said to him, "Rise and go to the street called Straight, and at the house of Judas look for a man of Tarsus named Saul, for behold, he is praying, and he has seen in a vision a man named Ananias come in and lay his hands on him so that he might regain his sight." But Ananias answered, "Lord, I have heard from many about this man, how much evil he has done to your saints at Jerusalem. And here he has authority from the chief priests to bind all who call on your name." But the Lord said to him, "Go, for he is a chosen instrument of mine to carry my name before the Gentiles and kings and the children of Israel. For I will show him how much he must suffer for the sake of my name." (Acts 9:3–16)

Can we build a house on two foundations if the first is laid properly and accurately? Did the twelve and Paul fail to lay that foundation? Is the revelation we have in the scriptures enough? Is it complete, accurate, and infallible? The answers to these questions are pivotal and will determine whether we value scripture.

We do not wonder that the Israelites, upon arriving in the promised land, no longer had manna coming down every morning to feed them. We understand that to have been a special miracle for a specific time to authenticate the ministry of Moses and later of Joshua before the people. So, how is it that we do not understand that the overabundance of miracles through the apostles was just for that time? God was using those miracles to authenticate the gospel of Jesus Christ; to prove the resurrection of his Son; and to validate the ministry and authority of the apostles and their writings, which we call the scripture of the New Testament.

Is it necessary when building a house to set up another foundation on the thirty-third floor?

When one builds a skyscraper or a house, there is only *one* foundation. No architect worth his salt would place a foundation on the ground level and then another one on the top floor. Jesus is the foundation and cornerstone of our faith upon which the prophets and apostles built the remaining foundation. The Church since has built upon the teachings of the apostles and prophets and it is upon their discourses that we discern what is true and what is false in our day. Since the ministry of the apostles was foundational and the foundation is the primary layer, there is no need for this authoritative office in our generation, as it was completed in the first century. What the Church is to do now is validate the teachings and doctrine from the pulpits opposite of what the scriptures teach. If they do not align themselves with the apostles' teachings, then we must discard them as false teachings.

Is the initial structure strong enough and sufficient enough if an expert architect has designed the plans?

If God is the Creator and Christ is the foundation of the Church, would we think that the foundation God laid was insufficient to maintain the building that is the Body of Christ? Of course not. Yet, we look to modern-day apostles and prophets as if God needs to lay the foundation again. They tell us the foundation is cracked and we are only recovering or repairing what has fallen apart. They say the principle of restorationism must be applied. However, if the foundation is faulty and Christ is the foundation, are you saying that Christ is faulty or unable to maintain purity in his Church? God forbid. His Body, the invisible and mystical Church, is now and forever will be pure. It is only the visible Church that fails, not the camp of the saints (cf. Matt 16:18 "the gates of Hades will not overcome it").

WHAT EVEN PENTECOSTALS DECLARED ABOUT THIS MOVEMENT

In 1949, the General Council of the Assemblies of God held in Seattle[4] said:

> The Council overwhelmingly approved a resolution that was prepared by a committee that dealt with the Latter Rain Movement. The resolution adopted disapproved of the following practices of the Latter Rain, and the action was made necessary as a result of the movement invading the Assembly of God churches:

---

4. Unknown, "Endtime Revival—Spirit-Led and Spirit-Controlled," Please see notes at bottom of article.

1. The overemphasis relative to imparting, identifying, bestowing, or confirming of gifts by the laying on of hands and prophecy.
2. The erroneous teaching that the Church is built on the foundation of present-day apostles and prophets.
3. The extreme teaching as advocated by the "New Order," regarding the confession of sin to man and deliverance as practiced, which claims prerogatives to human agency which belongs only to Christ.
4. The erroneous teaching concerning the impartation of the gift of languages as special equipment for missionary service.
5. The extreme and unscriptural practice of imparting or imposing personal leadings by the means of the gifts of utterance.
6. Such other wrestling and distortions of scripture interpretations which are in opposition to teachings and practices generally accepted among us.[5]

In a letter from the Executive Presbytery of the Assemblies of God (April 20, 1949), these observations were given. Some heresies just do not want to go away.

> The true test of any movement is whether or not it will stand up under the light of the word of God. We cannot depend alone upon the testimony of spiritual blessing, which many have claimed to have received under the "new order." When the "Jesus Only" issue swept the country in the years 1914–1917, there was a constant testimony that this was a revelation from God accompanied by great spiritual blessing. The movement was judged, however, not on the testimony of spiritual blessings, but on its adherence to the scriptures. When it was found that its claims did not conform to sound doctrine, its message was rejected. Dire calamities were predicted upon all who failed to "walk in the light" of that "revelation" but all predictions failed of fulfilment. We have heard similar predictions for failure to accept the "new order" teaching, which we regret exceedingly.

To my knowledge, this condemnation of the "new order" teaching has never been rescinded. Yet, Assemblies of God pastors will not challenge this doctrine. In fact, many actually promote it in their churches.

---

5. Menzies, *Anointed to Serve*.

> How shall we labor with any effect to build up the Church if we have no thorough knowledge of her history or fail to apprehend it from the proper point of observation? History is, and must ever continue to be, next to God's word, the richest foundation of wisdom and sweet guide to all successful practical activity.[6]

As the leading Pentecostal denomination globally, the Assemblies of God is an authoritative voice on many issues near and dear to Charismatics. So, it needs to be asked, why do they *ignore* this warning? Why are they insistent upon running after these apostles and prophets who by their own false and errant teachings prove themselves over and over again to be nothing more than charlatans and ego-driven power mongerers?

What was the Church built upon? Scripture answers us in Paul's letters to the churches in Asia Minor:

> According to the grace of God given to me, like a skilled master builder I laid a foundation, and someone else is building upon it. Let each one take care how he builds upon it. For no one can lay a foundation other than that which is laid, which is Jesus Christ. (1 Cor 3:10–11)

Paul says here that the foundation that was laid was and is Jesus Christ. Here the *building* or *superstructure* is raised *on* Christ the "foundation," laid by Paul. Later we read that the "lively stones" in 1 Peter 2:5 are the believers. However, the foundation (or rather cornerstone) is Jesus Christ and the remaining foundation is the apostles and prophets. Paul is warning the Corinthians of the erroneous teachings of the "super apostles." The foundation Paul is speaking of is the pure *doctrinal and practical teaching* of the Church. There were those teachers who succeeded Paul and added to his first teaching; not that they taught what was false, but their teaching was subtle and speculative rather than biblical reasoning. Paul is warning them *not* to add anything to the doctrinal and practical teachings of the apostles or prophets.

Many teach that revelatory knowledge is continuing today in the same way as that which was given to the prophets and apostles of old. They claim that it must be lined up with already revealed canonical scripture, but this only serves to make God's inscripturated voice now secondary, thereby creating a new criterion for revelation. Yet if the foundations were laid, as scripture teaches, then certain questions must be asked. Did

---

6. Schaff, "Preface to the Third Edition," *History of the Christian Church.*

Christ fail? Do we suppose that the revelation of Jesus was not sufficient to the apostles and therefore we need additional "revelations" today?

It should be asked whether the cornerstone has cracked. After the revelation was completed within the canon of the scriptures, known as the Old and New Testaments, did that canon falter? The interpretations may have faltered and failed and in some cases were completely obscured by men after their own interests. But does that mean the completed revelation we have in the Old and New Testaments is not sufficient to teach and to train, admonish, encourage, and correct, as Paul told Timothy (cf. 2 Tim 3:16–17)?

If there is continuing revelation, what we are saying is that there is no foundation upon which we can validate and authenticate those revelations. As the Archbishop of Canterbury, Thomas Cranmer, wrote on the holy scriptures:

> If there were any word of God beside the scripture, we could never be certain of God's word; and if we be uncertain of God's word, the devil might bring in among us a new word, a new doctrine, a new faith, a new church, a new God, yea himself to be a God. If the Church and the Christian faith did not stay itself upon the word of God certain, as upon a sure and strong foundation, no man could know whether he had a right faith, and whether he were in the true Church of Christ, or a synagogue of Satan.[7]

Further we read:

> So then you are no longer strangers and aliens, but you are fellow citizens with the saints and members of the household of God, built on the foundation of the apostles and prophets, Christ Jesus himself being the cornerstone, in whom the whole structure, being joined together, grows into a holy temple in the Lord. (Eph 2:19–21)

Scripture tells us that we are built on the apostles and prophets. What this means is that it is their teachings, the canonical teachings of the Old Testament prophets and the New Testament apostles (which Jesus promised would be exactly what he taught them), that are the final arbiters of what God is saying to his Church—always.

In verse twenty, the Church is compared to a building. The apostles and prophets are *the foundation* of that building. They may be so called in

---

7. Archbishop Thomas Cranmer, *Founders Said, Redemption.*

a secondary sense, Christ himself being the primary foundation, but we are rather to understand it as the doctrine delivered by the prophets of the Old Testament and the apostles of the New. It follows, *Jesus Christ himself being the chief cornerstone.* In him both Jews and Gentiles meet and constitute one Church, and Christ supports the building by his strength.

It is built upon the foundation of the apostles. In other words, their ministry involved validation of the ministry of Christ and inscripturation of revelation (see Matt 16:18). Christ himself, the only true foundation, was the grand subject of their ministry and spring of their inspiration. As one with him and his fellow workers, they too, in a symbolic sense, are called "foundations" (Rev 21:14). The "prophets" are joined with them closely, for the expression here is not "*foundations* of the apostles and *the* prophets," but "*foundations* of the apostles and *prophets.*" Though the apostles take the precedence (Luke 10:24), the doctrine of both is equal. He therefore appropriately shows regard to the claims of the Jews and Gentiles: "the prophets" representing the old Jewish dispensation (i.e., the Old Testament scripture) and "the apostles" the New Covenant.

Today's modern apostles and prophets take to themselves authority that *does not belong to them*. In doing so, they lower the integrity of the word of God, thereby calling into question the very words of our Lord in the above passages. They create a secondary tier for the word of God, separating it into the categories of "*logos*" and "*rhema.*"

Logos is normally used in two forms: with reference to the Son of God (cf. John 1:1) and with reference to the entire word of God. Rhema means "a saying." It refers to a particular portion of God's written revelation.[8] It is not, as the Charismatics would propose, a "now" word in their sense of a "new" word for the moment. It is the Holy Spirit applying specific verses to a specific issue that is being dealt with.

Logos to the modern-day apostles and prophets is the written word. Some even translate logos in John 1 to "dream." *In the beginning the "dream" was with God.* They tend to allegorize scripture, which leaves them with a vacuum that must be filled. They fill this with what they believe is a separate and distinct type of word from the Lord called rhema. Whereas scholars of Greek understand that rhema and logos are pretty much interchangeable, the modern-day apostles and prophets state that rhema is a "now word." Thus, rhema does not have to be found in scripture

---

8. Boice, *Acts: An Expositional Commentary,* 252.

because it is a general revelation of God. However, the scripture makes no differentiation between rhema and logos; they are synonymous. It is a dangerous thing to teach that there is ongoing revelation apart from the scriptures.

During the Reformation, those who were defending the faith fought hard to stand upon the scriptures *alone* as the only source of direction for faith and life and as the only divine source of revelation. Shall we head back to Rome and her continued revelations? God forbid.

As people of the written word, we must always remember that *experience must be judged in light of the scriptures*. Emotional interpretation, experiential learning, and basing truths on our "gut instinct" are all subjective. Truth is not subjective but objective. It does not need our experience to validate it, nor can it rest upon emotions that ebb and flow with circumstances and happenings around us. For the true believer, scripture is the *only* source of truth that can be validated and the only witness we are to go to as reliable.

However, we stand upon the shoulders of godly men who have gone before us and it is wise to remember how they exegete the scriptures. Though ultimately scripture rules over experience and interpretation, God has graciously given us teachers and pastors who rightly divide the word of truth so that we may know the difference between valid and invalid interpretation.

The fundamental elements of the scriptural position on prophets and apostles are:

1. The New Testament prophets and apostles were the givers of divine, inspired, infallible revelation to the first-century Church and each subsequent generation through their writings.

2. The offices of prophet and apostle and their corresponding gift (prophecy) were limited to the Jewish and apostolic era and have, with the close of those eras, been withdrawn from the Church.

3. When the writings of the New Testament were finished, all necessary revelation was completed, thereby removing the necessity of someone or a group to "hear from God" directly as now all his people could hear the word of the Lord in the same manner until the end of time.

Apostles/Prophets

Let us look now at what some pastors, preachers, and theologians throughout Church history have stated regarding the office of apostle and prophet.

J. A. Alexander, writing about Acts 13:1, says,

> Now there were in the church at Antioch prophets and teachers, Barnabas, Simeon who was called Niger, Lucius of Cyrene, Manaen a member of the court of Herod the tetrarch, and Saul.' Prophets and teachers ... i.e. either inspired teachers, as a single class, or inspired and uninspired teachers, as distinct classes. Or, still more probably than either, the two words are generic and specific terms, applied to the same persons, one denoting their divine authority, the other the precise way in which it was exercised.[9]

James M. Boice says,

> Apostles and prophets ... Some who have written about the gifts have tried to show that apostles and prophets are present today ... in these lists both apostle and prophet must be taken in their most technical sense. Therefore, apostles refer to those witnesses who were specifically commissioned by Christ to establish the church on a proper base, and prophets refer to those who received God's message (like prophets of old) and recorded it in the pages of what we call the New Testament. Neither one of these gifts exist today. We no longer have apostles or prophets in that sense.[10]

Robert L. Dabney says,

> The call of these particular classes (apostles and prophets) was extraordinary and by special revelation, suited to those days of Theophanies and inspiration. But those days have now ceased, and God governs his church exclusively by his providence, and the Holy Spirit applying the written word.[11]

And finally, we will look at what is said by a favorite preacher and author of the Charismatics and Pentecostals, D. Martin Lloyd-Jones.

> A prophet is one who receives a direct message from God. He is one to whom the truth is revealed directly by the Spirit—not as a result of reading the scripture or anything else, but by a direct message given, which he in turn is to impart to others ... They

---

9. Alexander, *The Acts of the Apostles*, 63.
10. Boice, *God & History*, 121.
11. Dabney, *Discussions: Evangelical and Theological*, 26–27.

had no New Testament scriptures then; neither the gospels nor the epistles were available to them; but there were these people who were given spiritual truth and understanding by direct revelation and were enabled to speak it. The prophet in the Old Testament did exactly the same. God revealed truth to him and enabled him to speak it. This is the characteristic of a prophet.[12]

Earlier we saw that the primary criterion for being an apostle was that the candidate must have seen the physically resurrected Jesus. A prima facie evidence for calling oneself an apostle is the necessity to have seen the Risen Lord. Peter and the other ten disciples saw him on Easter morning and the following weeks before his ascension. Paul saw him on the road to Damascus and later tells us in Galatians that he was taught by Christ himself and than went to the leaders in Jerusalem to validate the revelation Christ gave him and to authenticate what he had been taught.

Do we hold today's apostles and prophets to the same criteria? *Why not?* If these are the requirements that scripture lays down for these offices, why do we not hold to scripture? Why do we permit these apostles to move outside of what God has told us about them? Why do we permit them to take upon themselves mantles that do not belong to them?

It is because we have itching ears and do not take God's word at face value any longer. It is because we have been duped as a result of neglecting to acquaint ourselves with Church history. It is due to our lack of learning and reading about Church history that we have doomed ourselves to repeat it.

Paul states clearly to the Corinthians, "Am I not an apostle? Have I not seen Jesus our Lord? Are you not the result of my work in the Lord?" (1 Cor 9:1). Afterwards, Paul, when referring to the various resurrection appearances of Jesus, states, "Then he appeared to James, then to all the apostles, and last of all he appeared to me also, as to one abnormally born" (1 Cor 15:7–8). It is very clear from scripture these two things—first, that Paul saw the risen Savior and second that Paul was "the last" to whom Christ appeared.

The passages in 1 Corinthians 15 are important because they show that Paul was called as an apostle apart from the others, yet his authenticity as an apostle was proven in the same ways that Peter, James, and John were authenticated. There is, as stated before, a ring of finality in the Holy

---

12. Lloyd-Jones, *God's Way of Reconciliation: Studies in Ephesians, Chapter 2.*

Apostles/Prophets

Spirit writing that Paul was "the last." Paul's apostleship was not only authenticated by the Holy Spirit, but God also graciously condescended to validate it through the first apostles as Paul refers to it in Galatians 2:9.

These modern-day apostles and prophets have *not* had these two primary authenticating signs that would verify their office and yet they *take it to themselves* and demand that we approve of it while scripture clearly teaches otherwise. They place themselves into a position of authority that only those who had physically seen the Risen Christ could maintain. Even among those who had seen the Risen Savior, they were not all called apostles—those such as Mary, who had seen Jesus alive after his resurrection but did not have other apostolic office authenticating signs.

The apostles also were validated by maintaining infallibility with regard to the scriptures, which they penned. God had, through the apostles, given to his Church certain infallible sermons and specimens of scriptural interpretation. They had a God-given ability to apply Old Testament scripture in a binding and conclusive way, which is clearly seen in the summarizing of Church dogma and practice at the Jerusalem Council.

Augustine said, "In the Old Testament the New Testament was concealed and in the New Testament the Old revealed." If this is held to be true, as has been accepted for much of Christian history, then we must also be held to the interpretations of the apostles of the Old Testament texts as applied in the New. This then makes the Epistles the *only* successors to the apostles. Because of the disregard for the biblically outlined instructions for interpretation, many have wrested the scriptures to their own ruin. Charismatics and Pentecostals have brought in many varied and often weird interpretations and explanations for passages from the Bible because they have forgotten to apply the proper exegetical rules of interpretation to these passages. This is one reason they can assert the continuation of the apostolic and prophetic offices along with the "sign-gifts" of prophecy, tongues, and interpretation.

Jesus warned us that in the last days many would say they had been given a special "*anointing*" and would perform miracles and speak with power. Jesus also warned us that these would be rejected as those he did not ever know. Jesus further warned us that many would say they had seen Jesus, but we are not to believe them. Now, if these are the very warnings of Jesus, do we ignore them? Do we reject his very own teachings?

Too often we ignore and reject Jesus's teachings because we prefer to have our itching ears scratched by the latest pragmatic teaching instead of basing our faith upon the sure foundation of the word of God. It seems that the western mentality of instant gratification has trickled down into the Church. No longer is the time-consuming study of the scriptures and reading of the Church fathers, history of the Christian Church, or theological books and commentaries thought of as healthy disciplines and practices. Instead, one simply goes to a prophetic conference to be told what God is saying. It is always easier hear what you want to hear than to listen to what God has to say in the scriptures. It is much quicker to receive a word of knowledge or wisdom from someone else than to personally dig into the treasures of the word of God for doctrine, teaching, admonitions, exhortations, and correction. Christians today are, for the most part, lazy consumers gathering to themselves the trinkets and baubles from televangelists as a shortcut to godliness. May God withhold his judgment against the western Church with its "I want it yesterday" idle and indolent attitude and behavior.

The scriptures show that the apostles were specific men ordained for a unique office in a specific time period for the Church (Eph 2:20). "Having *been built* on the foundation of the apostles and prophets." Notice the past tense in the words, "*having been built.*" Once a foundation is laid, there is no need to lay it down again. The Church is "built upon" the foundation of the apostles and prophets. And these men were built upon Jesus Christ, who is himself the chief cornerstone. Those who claim apostolic authority today are attempting to rebuild the foundation that has *already been laid and built*. In Ephesians 4:11 Paul writes, "And he himself gave some to be apostles and prophets, some evangelists and some pastors and teachers . . ." There is within that verse a finality of the office. It does not say that God continually gives, but that He "gave," which is past tense. Because there is no distinction in this passage as to which office is continual and which is not, it must be read in view of Ephesians 2:20 where Paul delineates that the apostles and prophets are the foundation. No builder ever places a foundation a second time in a building. Foundations are once for all tasks. Pastors and teachers continue because they are not foundational offices but instead are leaders and rulers over the congregations after the apostles were gone, but the foundation does not need to be re-laid.

The apostles wrote down the doctrinal teaching for the Church as well as the historical events of Christ's birth, life, death, resurrection, and ascension.

Let Us Reason Ministries writes:

Apostles/Prophets

> If there are apostles today in the sense of the Church's origins then of necessity there would have to be new revelation. This would have to be included as scripture because apostolic revelation is authoritative and infallible. It would then be on the same level as our Bible.[13]

This is similar to what the Mormon Church and Jehovah's Witnesses claim and many other cult groups. To say we have modern-day apostles like Peter, John, James, and Paul is to say scripture is still being written. This leads to the rejecting or diminishing of that which was written by the apostles who were appointed by Jesus. As John writes in his first letter:

> That which was from the beginning, which we have heard, which we have seen with our eyes, which we have looked upon, and our hands have handled, concerning the word of life—the life was manifested, and we have seen, and bear witness, and declare to you that eternal life which was with the Father and was manifested to us—that which we have seen and heard we declare to you, that you also may have fellowship with us; and truly our fellowship is with the Father and with His Son Jesus Christ. And these things we write to you that your joy may be full. (1 John 1:1–4)

Great men of the Christian Church such as Irenaeus, Augustine, Luther, Calvin, Edwards, great theologians like Charles Hodge, Theodore Beza, Martin Chemnitz, and others were content to build upon the foundation already laid by the original apostles. Not one of these men claimed the office of apostle. The only apostles mentioned in Church history after the Bible was finished were false ones.

The office of apostle was the most important gift given to the Church after Christ ascended. However, it was a temporary office and as such no longer continues. Their task was to proclaim the gospel of Jesus Christ, write the life of Christ down in the gospels, and lay out the doctrines of the Church. They completed their task and therefore God's word is complete, so no new revelation is needed. While the Lord does speak to us today through his word and the sacraments, he does not give any new revelation or doctrine since it has been delivered and completed. God speaks through his word, the preaching of his word, and the illumination of the Holy Spirit.

---

13. Oppenheimer, "Apostles and Prophets." Grateful recognition is given to the content of this website from which the previous explanations have been based in part.

Paul called himself the least of all apostles because he knew that he had previously persecuted the Church. He would never lord his authority over churches but would often implore them to follow the teachings of the other apostles as their foundation of faith.

Paul also said that he was one born "out of time." This is a birth reference to one who is not born in the normal order but is born later. Paul was humbled by this calling and often referred to himself as the least of all apostles: *not meant to be called an apostle.* "He referred to himself as the least because he was the last of them; called at the end to the office, and not worthy to be called an apostle, to have either the office or the title, because he had been *a persecutor of the church of God.*"[14] This reference also teaches us that he was the last of the apostles. If he was the last, which the scripture teaches us, why then do we say there are apostles today?

We place today's teachings over and above the clear teachings of God's word. This is a dangerous place to stand because if the word of God is not sure—if it is not without error or if it fails or falters in any respect—then we cannot rely upon it for any truth.

We read here that Paul was the last of the apostles in the revelatory and foundational sense. The question is whether these "apostles" in the true sense of the term, as those who still receive direct propositional revelation from God, exist beyond the time of the twelve apostles and Paul—those who founded the Church upon the chief cornerstone, Jesus Christ.

Paul clearly marks himself out to be the *last* of this type of apostle. And we must admit that the prevalent and loose usage of the word of "apostle" has obscured the uniqueness of the twelve and Paul. It would have been better if the word "missionary" had been used in their place.

He notes that he did not sit under the three years of teaching by Jesus. However, his conversion was ordained by God for that specific time which turned him from a persecutor of the Church to a propagator of its Lord and Savior, Jesus Christ. It changed Paul from an oppressor to an apostle. If Paul describes himself as the "last" of the apostles, and this statement is found in the written word of God, then we must then base our understanding of this office as having had a final apostle and therefore no more in this revelatory office will ever exist. Either all of Paul's writings that have come down to us in scripture are authoritative, infallible,

---

14. Ibid.

inerrant, and inspired or we drag ourselves into a paradox that cannot be solved. How can we hold to Sola Scriptura and yet affirm modern revelation and inscripturation?

To state that some of Paul's writings were his own personal understanding or his own personal comments and were not under the direct control of the Holy Spirit as he wrote them is to call not just some but all of Paul's writings into question. If we do that, we then call Peter's writings into question because he affirms the inspiration of Paul's writings in his own. This then calls us to question the gospel of Mark, as history states it was Peter's secretary, Mark, who wrote it under the direction of Peter. This brings us to the same view as higher criticism and thereby destroys the authority of God's word. Is the scripture merely the fanciful writings of enthusiastic but deluded men or the very authoritative word of God himself?

Perhaps part of the problem lies in having an obscure understanding of what the apostolic office actually is. Let us go on then to briefly understanding why the apostolic gifting existed.

Scripture is clear that miracles were for signs of authentication with regard to the gospel message and seals of the apostles' authority. Benjamin B. Warfield states clearly at the beginning of his work *Counterfeit Miracles* the following:

> The extraordinary gifts of the Spirit, prophecy, tongues, miracles on demand or instantaneous miracles, including raising of the dead at a command, were distinctively the authentication of the apostles. They were part of the credentials of the apostles as the authoritative agents of God in founding the church. Their function, therefore, confined them to distinctively the Apostolic Church, and they necessarily passed away with it.[15]

The gifts of miracle working or powers were never were intended to continue on indefinitely, as the extreme faith healer of today contends, since they were confined to the apostolic age, and to a very narrow circle even then. As stated previously, these were foundational gifts for the establishment of the Church of Christ which now included not only Jewish believers but also Gentiles of every tongue and tribe.

---

15. Warfield, *Counterfeit Miracles*, 5–6.

A Modern Ninety-Five

ADDENDUM

While on vacation as I was writing this book, I received an e-mail from a prominent Charismatic/Pentecostal magazine. The story it told was so disturbing that it must be included in this chapter. Though the writer has not revealed who this "more than an apostle" is, it is important to know that when men and women begin to read their own opinions into the scriptures, it is never too long before they fall for the original lie of Satan, "You will be like God" (Gen 3:5).

> It gets worse, if you can believe it. At a Charismatic conference in an East Coast city recently, a pastor stood on a stage in front of a large crowd and smugly announced that the guest speaker was "more than an apostle." Then the host asked everyone to bow down to the person, claiming that this posture was necessary to release God's power.
>
> "This is the only way you can receive this kind of anointing!" the host declared, bowing in front of the speaker. Immediately, about 80 percent of the audience fell prostrate on the floor. The few who were uncomfortable with the weird spiritual control in the room either walked out or stood in silent protest.[16]

Though the fact that this preacher demands worship, which is only to be given to God, is shocking, what is more *appalling* is that 80 percent "fell prostrate" before a human and none spoke out against this at that conference; there was only silent protestation. Is there no one who will take a stand and warn the church about these people? Is there no one who will challenge them publically and charge them face-to-face to bow their knees to the only wise and sovereign God? Does the church think this will just go away if it is ignored long enough? It's time, Church, to declare the whole counsel of God, to maintain doctrinal integrity, to stand by the revealed word of God, and to oust these charlatans.

---

16 Grady, "Fire in My Bones."

2

Can We Know Absolute Truth?

13. *Christians are to be taught that the word of God is complete; there are no new revelations.*

14. *We seek words of knowledge and wisdom when God has provided both sufficiently in his written word and in the word of God incarnate—Jesus Christ.*

15. *Christians are to be taught that the word of God is sufficient; there is no need to add anything to it and if one does, one adds to oneself the condemnations found therein.*

16. *Christians are to be taught that the word of God is authoritative; all experiences are to be examined in the light of holy scripture and if true, there will be no shadows, but if false, they are to be rejected no matter how much they may have influenced someone's faith.*

17. *Christians are to be taught the very word of God is their only source of prophetic words both now and forevermore.*

18. *Christians are to be taught that we deny any creed, council, or individual that may bind a Christian's conscience, claims that the Holy Spirit speaks independently of or contrary to what is set forth in the Bible, or claims that personal spiritual experience can ever be a vehicle of revelation.*

19. *Yet, how does someone do what he or she does not know to be right? Creeds tell us truth in a concise and organized manner, and the Bible itself is full of its own statements of faith.*

20. *The Lord our God is one God. Hallelujah!*

21. *"All scripture is breathed out by God and profitable for teaching, for reproof, for correction, and for training in righteousness, that the man of God may be competent, equipped for every good work" (2 Tim 3:16–17) is the biblical mandate that includes the teaching that doctrine is good for us.*

22. *"He was manifested in the flesh, vindicated by the Spirit, seen by angels, proclaimed among the nations, believed on in the world, taken up in glory" (1 Tim 3:16) is a biblical declaration of the deity and humanity of Jesus, thereby being in itself one of the earliest creeds.*

23. *The scriptures are used to prove sermon points instead of sermons built upon the scriptures.*

24. *Scripture tells us that all things are to be held in the light of God's word.*

25. *Therefore, Christians are to be sufficiently taught the word of God so that they do not fall into the emotional hyperventalisms of today's Charismatic and "yappaphilic" preachers.*

The question at the heading of the chapter asks the question, "Can we know truth?" Better still should be asked, "Is there objective truth in this world and is it the final truth?"

While the post-modernists will state that all truth is truth while at the same time agreeing that there is no absolute truth, most people will say that there is truth out there. How then are people to know what is true? There must be one who has taught absolute, objective truth. And if that truth has been taught, where are we to find it? The Koran? The Communist Manifesto? The Bhagavad-Gita? The Bible?

It would be a circular argument to distinguish that "for the Christian (alone) objective truth is found in the Bible." After all, if the Bible is the sole source of absolute truth, then it is not distinguished singularly for the Christian alone but is truth for *all* humanity.

Since God has given us the truth—has written it down for us by the hands of prophets and apostles who were also kings, fishermen, shepherds, and others—we must look at the scriptures for the answer to all our questions. There is no safer place to go than to the written word of God for the plumb line by which we determine the validity and veracity of teachings that are being proclaimed; it is the weight by which all teaching is measured and found to be true or false. The Bible is the hammer that breaks away the lies of the flesh, the world, and the devil and opens up the core of men and women to the truth of God that lies within Christ himself. It is through scripture that God has revealed himself for men and women to know who he is, what he requires, and what he has done to fulfill his own requirements.

All this is stated first so that those reading this work will understand that all subsequent truths must first be examined under the microscope of the biblical texts to see if they remain faithful in substance and essence. If the teaching is found to not line up the scripture, the teacher is to be confronted in love. If he or she remains unrepentant, his or her teachings are to be exposed for the error and heresy they would endeavor to bring into the Church. Sincerity is no substitute for scriptural accuracy.

Unfortunately, those who were supposed to watch the gates became themselves enticed by the false teachings, thinking they were not as dangerous as they were warned to be, and they let the wolves into the sheepfold (i.e., the visible Church). These ravenous creatures have devastated the Church. What was known to be false is now openly accepted and lovingly embraced by even those who once warned against such horror.

It is therefore necessary to once again, or maybe for some for the first time, learn the special place the written word of God holds in this world and how all other supposed truths are to be examined by it.

WHAT IS THE WORD OF GOD?

The word of God is the revelatory and written message given to mankind that delineates the redemptive purposes of God through the ministry of Jesus Christ, the living word. It is God's revelation to mankind of the history of redemption that is only found in completion in Jesus of Nazareth. This word of God is the only revelation whereby we are given objective truth.

REVELATION IS COMPLETE AND PERFECT

Just because someone claims to have had a "revelation" or "religious experience" does not validate the content of that experience, *nor does it prove the experience to be true in and of itself.* The experience could either be psychosomatic or a bad reaction to rotten food or perhaps even a chemical imbalance within the person experiencing the revelation. Revelations must be cohesive, revealing similar things, and not contradictory. For instance, if one says that God has revealed himself as a god who lives on another plant, as the Word of Faith proponents do ("copy of the mother planet"[1]), and another says that God dwells in heaven, both revelations cannot be correct, and therefore one of them is a false religious experience.

Since religious experience varies around the globe, we cannot automatically accept these revelations since many *contradict each other on the most foundational level*. One says that there are a thousand gods, another that there is one, still another that God is female and another that God is neither male nor female. Unless we agree with the illogical statement, "All roads lead to God," we can never rationally accept the myriad disagreeing and opposite revelations as if they come from the same source. All cannot be true if all do not inherently agree. All could be false, but not all can be true because many "religious experiences" are diametrically opposed to each other. This is why a *singular source of revelation is needed*.

SINGLE SOURCE OF REVELATION NEEDED

So what can be done? A standard of revelation must be set as the standard by which to test and evaluate all religious experiences—not just purportedly Christian ones. This standard must be *free from error* and contradiction in order to be the starting point of testing and examining any and all "religious experiences." The religious experience then must be examined in light of a singular source to prove its authenticity and validity. A person must not be doubted as to whether or not he or she truly and actually experienced something, but the content of that experience must be evaluated to see whether it is true. The standard must be held to no matter the experience, for the experience must be tested in the light of the standard—the scriptures. If the standard is tested in light of the experience, one will fall into gross error. Therefore, the standard by which religious experience is tested must be trustworthy bibliographically, internally, externally, and critically. If the religious experience matches that of the standard, it may then be deemed valid and authentic. If, however, the experience does not cohere with the standard set forth, it must be rejected as a valid experience. The testimony that a person experienced

---

1. Kenneth Copeland, "Side 1," in *Spirit, Soul, and Body Audio Tape # 01-0601*.

"something" is not invalidated; only the content of that "religious experience" is proven to be untrustworthy and false.

God has revealed himself in two very different ways—natural or general revelation and supernatural revelation, which is often called scripture. Romans 1 describes the effect that total depravity had upon man. He is incapable of seeing God in nature and in his fellow human beings as those who are made in the image of God.

Natural or general revelation was not the complete picture of God for humanity as it was imperfect, weak, limited, and natural and due to the Fall, man has corrupted it. Natural revelation is imperfect in that it only reveals to us that there is a God, but not who he is or even that he is a personal Creator and loving Father. Because of this, knowing that there is a Creator, natural revelation is weak because it brings across a more deist type of God who is the master planner or cosmic designer or "higher power." Yet this revelation does not show humanity the loving, personal nature of this Creator, and even more so, it does not teach us about the gracious promises of redemption and the remission of sins. This natural revelation leaves us with a Creator who has made us but is not involved with us in our daily lives and in providential ways.

Natural revelation is fatally inadequate. We cannot read God's will in the stars or in ourselves. Because of this limitation, God may be feared and admired, but there is no true worship because no one knows what his requirements are or what his blessings might be. So the unregenerate heart is left with a God who is an angry Creator and nothing more.

Because mankind is dead in sins and trespasses through the Adamic fall, man cannot ascend to God and true spirituality. Since we are dead spiritually, the ability to understand and know God is rendered void as we blindly feel our way around the universe for something we neither understand nor can make contact with. Even if mankind did come to hear about the true God, it cannot respond due to spiritual inability.

SPECIAL REVELATION

It therefore was God's design from the beginning to reveal himself to the elect in a special but diverse way. Through supernatural (or outside nature) revelation, God began to show himself to men and women. This special revelation was first through direct revelation as he spoke to Adam, Seth, Methuselah, and Noah, revealing his plans to them one on one.

Later, God would speak to Moses directly. Moses began to write down the record of this special revelation for generations to come. So inscripturation, the process of writing down infallible revelation, began with Moses and continued with other men who were given the Spirit to guarantee they would make no mistake.

Within this special revelation, a crimson thread was woven into the very woof of the fabric, tracing itself through every line; this crimson thread was the promise of a redeemer who would undo what Adam had done. This specific revelation was God's plan of salvation. As God began to reveal more and more this eternal plan of salvation, he began to reveal the promises and prophecies about this Messiah. Various men were used of God to record the promises so that when the Messiah finally came, those who had been waiting would recognize him.

Through special revelation, men and women came to know God for who he is—his promises, his requirements, and his plan of salvation. God began to show them that he alone is God and there is none other beside him. He began to show that he was One that the Shema talks about, "Hear, O Israel, the Lord is One." While others worshipped a multiplicity of gods, the one true God revealed himself progressively as Father, Son, and Holy Spirit to his people. The almighty God was unfolding himself gradually until the time of Jesus Christ when at last he spoke to us "through his Son," the final word.

Redemptive revelation became the focus of God's special revelation for the elect, beginning with those among Abraham's descendents who were of the true Israel and at the time of Christ and the apostles, the elect Gentiles, some from every tongue, tribe, and nation, as many as the Lord our God would call until the return of Jesus, the Son of the living God. Through covenants God began to give glimpses and pictures of the final redemption that he would work out in the life, death, and resurrection of his Son, Jesus.

It was in the historic and progressive dealings of God with his people that men and women were brought into that salvation he planned before the foundation of the world. All of this was revealed through direct revelation to those who would inscripturate the word of God for the following generations. Through word and deed, the Fall, the Flood, the parting of the Red Sea, the giving of water from the rock (which later Paul explains was a picture of Jesus Christ and the living water we receive from him), and other things, God showed his plan of salvation in picture form—but always with prophetic explanation.

The law given through Moses was to teach us that none could ever be perfect in God's eyes and therefore a Savior would be needed to fulfill the law for us and impute that righteousness to our account in order that we may enjoy the blessings of eternal life with the Father. But this giving of word and deed would culminate in Jesus Christ and be fulfilled, completed, and perfected in the salvation work of Christ through his life, death, and resurrection.

Since Christ performed his task of redemption for the elect, that would necessitate a ceasing of the direct revelation, since all prior to Christ pointed to Christ and afterwards, which was explained by the apostles. If Christ was the culmination, the pinnacle of revelation, there would no longer be a need for further prophecies or direct words from God, since the Holy Spirit himself declares that Jesus is the final word. And since Christ is the final word through whom God speaks, why would there ever need to be another "word from the Lord" as so many teach today? Either revelation was completed in, through, and by Christ or the very scriptures that we read are incorrect. And if the scriptures are incorrect, then what part can we trust to be absolute truth, and then how do we determine what is accurate and what is not? But the scriptures clearly state that no further prophetic word would be given, nor is it needed, for Peter tells us by the Holy Spirit that all we need for life and godliness we already have and we have it in the written word, which tells us of the final word, Jesus Christ, the only begotten Son of the living God (cf. John 1:1).

SCRIPTURE: WHAT MAKES IT "SPECIAL"?

There are several aspects that determine why we call scripture God's special and propositional revelation. Terms such as inerrant, inspired, and infallible are used to describe different aspects that make the Bible unique and the sole authority for faith, life, and godliness—in fact for all things! It is important to understand the specialness of scripture in order to discern the movements in the Church today that push continual revelation and how that tears down the authority of scripture. So the question is, "What makes the Bible 'special'?"

First and foremost we must understand that the Bible is the inspired word of God. The sixty-six books that are contained in it are *not* the words of men about *God, but are the word of God about himself, his plan, his purposes, and his redemptive scheme to mankind.* What is meant by inspired is best understood by defining the term that scripture itself uses: *theopneustos* (God-breathed).

> All scripture is breathed out by God and profitable for teaching, for reproof, for correction, and for training in righteousness. (2 Tim 3:16)

The term "breathed out" is "divinely breathed by God." Just as God breathed life into Adam, so Paul states that the breath of God gives the life of scripture. We do not take this literally since God is not man that he would need to breathe, but we take it to mean that the very life of God is within scripture in a special sense. Peter says, "For no prophecy was ever produced by the will of man, but men spoke from God as they were carried along by the Holy Spirit" and therefore we understand that these were not the words of man recording their own ideas or thoughts, but they were directed by the Spirit of God who divinely wrought their words, keeping them free from all error.

Now, it is common for folks to misunderstand what Paul is saying here, as if he is simply saying that the scriptures exist on a slightly higher plane than the "normal" words of men; that is not what he taught. He used the Greek term theopneustos, which means "God-breathed" or "breathed out by God," and this tells us that the very scriptures themselves are the creation of God, reflecting his very breath, his very speaking. Matthew Henry comments on the passage from 2 Timothy:

> That the scripture was given by inspiration of God appears from the majesty of its style,—from the truth, purity, and sublimity, of the doctrines contained in it,—from the harmony of its several parts,—from its power and efficacy on the minds of multitudes that converse with it,—from the accomplishment of many prophecies relating to things beyond all human foresight,—and from the uncontrollable miracles that were wrought in proof of its divine original: *God also bearing them witness, both with signs and wonders, and with divers miracles and gifts of the Holy Ghost, according to his own will.* (Heb 2:4)

Any "word" given by God must be held as being divinely inspired—that is, breathed out by God (not from the will of man) and therefore infallible. Paul intended to teach infallibility by using "theopneustos." We will see later why this is crucial in discerning what is claimed to be direct and special revelation by God in today's Charismatic/Pentecostal, Word of Faith, and New Apostolic Reformation camps and why they cannot claim this to be true and are therefore deceiving the nations, giving them words that are not from the Lord but from either their own vain imaginations or the pit of hell itself. They cannot be true because they have been proven to not be infallible or in agreement with the infallible scriptures.

We will see later why the above statement is crucial in discerning what are claimed to be revelations by God in today's Charismatic/Pentecostal, Word of Faith, and New Apostolic Reformation camps. We will look at the biblical reasons why they cannot claim this to be true and are therefore deceiving the nations by giving them "words" that are not from the Lord but from either their own vain imaginations or the pit of hell itself.

> Behold, I am against the Prophets, declares the LORD, who use their tongues and declare, "Declares the LORD." Behold, I am against those who prophesy lying dreams, declares the LORD, and who tell them and lead my people astray by their lies and their recklessness, when I did not send them or charge them. So they do not profit this people at all, declares the LORD. (Jer 23:31–32)

God superintended the human authors so that using their own individual personalities, they composed and recorded without error his revelation to man in the words of the original manuscripts. These manuscripts have been preserved for us down through the ages.

How do we know that the Bible was divinely inspired? God has graciously condescended to our need by giving us several aspects to defend the inspiration of the scriptures.

First, we have the testimony of human authors. The question that arises at this point is whether the Bible is merely a product of human creativity. Since the majority of the writers were unlearned men and not great classical philosophers, this is highly unlikely. Some were fishermen, farmers, and tax collectors, while very few were educated men such as Moses, Isaiah, and Paul. Yet they wrote with absolute confidence that what they recorded was the word of God himself. They did not doubt that what they were writing was God's word, his prophetic utterances, his promises, and his plan of redemption.

One then asks: could they have been wrong? Well, to answer that one must consider the context of scripture. How could common men write something as magnificent as the Bible? It is so magnificent that it has been studied throughout history because of its unmatched literary significance. No other proclaimed "divine" book has ever compared with the Bible. Read the writings of Confucius, Mohammed, or the Hindu religions and you will not find the continuity, beauty, or reverence as is found in the holy scriptures. When Peter and John went before the Sanhedrin in Jerusalem, Peter said, "Neither is there salvation in any other; for there is no other name under heaven given among men, whereby we must be saved" (Acts 4:12). Scripture then records that the men of the Sanhedrin "perceived that they [Peter and John] were unlearned and ignorant men *and* marveled; and they took knowledge of them, that they had been with Jesus" (Acts 4:13–20).

Jesus had a very high view of the Old Testament, referring to it on numerous occasions. He refers to events such as the Flood and Jonah as actual historical occurrences and not mythological stories. Jesus revered the law and in fact stated that he did not come to do away with it but to actually fulfill it.

When Jesus speaks of the creation of Adam and Eve, he is teaching about adultery and divorce. He is dealing with an actual difficulty and not some theoretical one and therefore refers to an actual historical event to teach people about marriage. With Noah and the ark, Jesus is speaking of a future historical event, his second coming, and refers to a past historical event as proof positive that the judgements will occur in the future upon his return. As Jesus is teaching about his upcoming crucifixion and subsequent resurrection, he does not use an analogy from nature but refers once again to an historical event as a true event to prove that he will rise from the dead, this time utilizing the historical event of Jonah and the great fish. In all these passages Jesus refers to these biblical events as having actually taken place and not as some quaint "Sunday school" story we can dismiss when we grow older. Jesus actually validates these stories by utilizing their historicity as evidence for his teachings, the resurrection, and the second coming.

One of the first things that one observes from the encounter that Jesus had with the devil in the wilderness is that there was no one else around. This is key, because as the devil begins to test Jesus by quoting verses from the Old Testament, Jesus does not say anything against the passages but refers to them as the very words of God. Jesus could very well have said that these texts were not the inspired word of God and no one would have been the wiser, because no one else witnessed these events. However, Jesus's response shows how dangerous it is to wrest a text out of context and twist it to one's own definitions or presuppositions. Jesus emphatically uses the Bible for his own response against the twisting of the scriptures by the devil. This should teach us that the view Jesus held about these texts is that the entire Old Testament is God-breathed, inerrant, and infallible and not to be toyed with or twisted to one's own purposes. One must, when reading the texts of the prophets and other writers of the Old Testament, recognize that they are not colored by culturally shaded glasses, but in their entirety they are the word of God to mankind. The Old Testament texts, though written by different men from different cultural backgrounds and at different times, are nonetheless the inspired, inerrant word of God.

We have at least two clear passages where Jesus places his stamp of approval upon the text of the New Testament prior to them being written. John 14:26–27 states:

> But the helper, the Holy Spirit, whom the Father will send in my name, he will teach you all things and bring to your remembrance all that I have said to you. Peace I leave with you; my peace I give to you. Not as the world gives do I give to you. Let not your hearts be troubled, neither let them be afraid.

He then teaches in John 16:12–15:

> I still have many things to say to you, but you cannot bear them now. When the Spirit of truth comes, he will guide you into all the truth, for he will not speak on his own authority, but whatever he hears he will speak, and he will declare to you the things that are to come. He will glorify me, for he will take what is mine and declare it to you. All that the Father has is mine; therefore I said that he will take what is mine and declare it to you.

What Jesus is saying is that he approves of all the apostles will teach after the resurrection because it will come from the Holy Spirit. Jesus tells the disciples that the Spirit will teach them and cause them to remember everything so that they may in turn teach other believers. Jesus tells them that the Spirit of truth will remind them of the true sayings of Jesus and that they will not have to rely upon their own fallible recall but upon the infallible and inerrant total recall by the Spirit of God.

Therefore, Peter refers to Paul's writings as scripture, thereby affording to it the status of inspired, infallible, inerrant, and authoritative for the believer and fulfilling the words of Jesus with regard to the writings of the apostles; they would be equivalent in validity, authority, infallibility, and inerrancy, equally inspired as the Old Testament writings.

> And count the patience of our Lord as salvation, just as our beloved brother Paul also wrote to you according to the wisdom given him, as he does in all his letters when he speaks in them of these matters. There are some things in them that are hard to understand, which the ignorant and unstable twist to their own destruction, as they do the other scriptures. (2 Pet 3:15–16)

WHAT MAKES THE WRITTEN WORD SPECIAL?

The scriptures are special in that they are the *only* infallible book. Infallibility simply means that the Bible does not teach error and cannot teach error in anything that it affirms or denies. In order to study God, we must approach the Bible with the proper understanding, which is that the Bible in all sixty-six books is infallible and without error, being God's direct revelation to elect mankind.

The reasoning behind this is that God cannot err. It is impossible for God to lie (cf. Heb 6:18); God cannot deny himself (2 Tim 2:13); God himself is truth (cf. John 14:6); God is not fallen as man and therefore cannot lie (cf. Num 23:19). God has breathed his word, which is his mind, which is true and therefore is truth (cf. John 17:17 and Ps 119:160). God therefore validates his own word to be infallible—inspired and inerrant.

However, to further strengthen the hearts of believers, there is also a historical basis for infallibility. The Bible is actually historically accurate. Each time archeologists attempt to find something wrong with stories and events in the Bible, the archeological finds end up validating the biblical record. That God would maintain the validity of small events within the context of scripture should embolden our trust in his word as that which is infallible—safe to believe in.

There are over fifty-five hundred manuscripts or manuscript fragments can be compared to one another and provide an accurate picture of how the original texts read. Of the over twenty thousand lines of text in the New Testament manuscripts, only forty lines can be questioned and not one of them pertains to major or even secondary doctrine, but more to names of people and places. Compare that to the Iliad, which has 15,600 lines and 764 are called into question.[2] And, as we have gone through above, there is the internal verification of Jesus, who called the Old Testament the word of God (John 10:35).

The biblical basis for infallibility lies in its divine authority primarily. Within the text are numerous self-authenticating phrases such as, "It is written," "The Spirit said," and "The Lord spoke." These all have to do with the verification of the divinely inspired nature of the word of God. Though some claim these phrases today in churches with their "utterances," as we have seen, they would have to be 100 percent perfect 100 percent of the time to be authentic, direct revelations from God. This would clearly contradict what God has written in his word about continued revelation and would void the infallibility of scripture because it would show God to either be a liar or just plain forgetful. Since God's word is unbreakable (cf. John 10:35), continued prophecy and revelations could not occur because they would go counter to what God has revealed in his written word.

Also, continued revelation would make God's word perishable because no one keeps track of what God is saying in all these meetings and therefore they perish with the ending of the meetings. Since there are no continued records of what God is "saying today," one must either place these "words" in a secondary place next to scripture or state that the word of God is an open cannon subject to adjustments and additions. Since no one records these "words" of the Lord for the general people of God, what can we make of them? Would God not want all his people to hear his word throughout the world? Are these special revelations only for special congregations? Does God favor one church over another? Or do we follow the steps of Rome and equate these revelations with scripture and accord to them what only belongs to the written word of God—infallibility, inerrancy, and inspiration.

Though God could have used other means to reveal himself, in his sovereignty he chose to communicate his plan of salvation through the *written word*. This certainly providentially preserves God's communication to his people, leaving them a permanent witness to what he has spoken and a standard by which to believe and live. But certainly this word

---

2. House and Carle, *Doctrine Twisting: How Core Biblical Truths Are Distorted*, 23.

must have come to a culminating point wherein all that God desired to reveal to his people would then end. That God's word is "living and active, sharper than any two-edged sword, piercing to the division of soul and of spirit, of joints and of marrow, and discerning the thoughts and intentions of the heart," teaches us that his word is not dry bones to the spiritually alive. It is vibrant and active and the only source of life for the believer who must feast on it as the Israelites did daily on the manna sent from above.

THE AUTHORITY OF SCRIPTURE

Now that we have studied how God has spoken his word through direct revelation and maintained the proclamation of it so that it is without error and teaches only truth, we move on to the authority of scripture for all.

The call during the Reformation was Sola Scriptura, scripture alone. Among the key issues the reformers were battling was the teaching by the Roman Catholic church that God still speaks today either through the traditions, which were claimed to be inspired and infallible, thereby holding authority and rule over believers, or through the pope's pronouncements of binding doctrine *ex cathedra*. The Reformers maintained that the only source of revelation was to be found in the written word of God as handed down by the prophets and apostles and acknowledged by Church councils. Scripture teaches us that the only source of revelation is found within itself. It is above the traditions of man and therefore all who speak for the Lord must submit to the teachings and doctrines contained within. To go outside of scripture is "neither right nor safe," as man's words have too often proved unfounded and unstable.

This puts the written scriptures in a unique position for it is what we call the normative authority for all teachings, commentaries, sermons and homilies, devotionals, and exhortations. If a teaching is found to have not been taught within scripture, or historically held as a revealed truth, it must be discarded no matter how much it may have helped someone. Because of its authority, it alone binds the consciences of men and women by revealing God and teaching us about him.

It is in fact the simplicity of the Bible or the perspicuity (self-articulating and defining) of scripture that upholds the authority of the word of God. God, who has revealed himself, has not revealed himself in difficulties but in the simplicity of scripture. The greatest need of mankind is salvation and therefore God has revealed the important things in a plain and simple manner.

The sufficiency of scripture assures us that there is no need for another infallible teaching authority or "special anointing." All that is necessary to know for salvation and for living a holy life is contained perfectly and in *full* in the scriptures. Peter, by the Holy Spirit, reminded the believers that all they needed for life and for godliness they had received:

> His divine power has granted to us all things that pertain to life and Godliness, through the knowledge of him who called us to his own glory and excellence, by which he has granted to us his precious and very great promises, so that through them you may become partakers of the divine nature, having escaped from the corruption that is in the world because of sinful desire. (2 Pet 1:3–4)

Peter marks out that his divine power comes through the knowledge of Christ that is plainly revealed through the promises given to us *solely in the written word of God*. Therefore, scripture is the *complete* revelation of God's plan of redemption and no further "word from the Lord" is necessary, nor are they to be sought after. Visions and dreams are no longer needed, nor are special "ministers" because scripture contains everything and is complete.

Throughout Church history, the greatest preachers have been those who have recognized that they have no authority in themselves. They have seen their task as being to explain the words of scripture and apply them clearly to the lives of their hearers. They have not drawn their power from the proclamation of their own Christian experiences or the experiences of others. They have not drawn their power from their own opinions, creative ideas, or speaking skills. Theirs is the power of the Holy Spirit and the power of the word of God.

Scripture alone is sufficient to give us the information needed concerning God and salvation. Though confessions, creeds, commentaries, and sermons inform and guide us, they are *not equal* in authority to *scripture*. In conclusion, we see that the number of manuscripts validate the message of the Bible. We have learned that the Bible is the sole source of the redemptive message to mankind and the only true word of God. We have learned that the Bible is without error, is God-breathed, holds authority over us, is unique in its message and composition, is *not* difficult to understand, and is sufficient to guide us in life and godliness. I trust that if your Bible gathered dust before, it will now be a staple in your daily spiritual nourishment. It is my prayer that you will call to account all those who promote the continued revelations and prophetic utterances and that if caught in this heresy will, by God's grace alone, be removed from it and brought to the truth that is contained solely in the written word of God, which, as my husband states, has a *back cover*.

For review, let us look at the singular place of scripture as defined by the Reformers as *Sola Scriptura (scripture alone)*.

First, the word of God is complete. But what is the word of God? Is it some prophetic word from the Lord that some modern-day apostle is giving? No! It is found in the written word of God. This word has stood the test of time, has survived burnings and banishment, and still speaks to us today. You want a "word" from the Lord, pick up your Bible.

But I must warn you; the scriptures will take you beyond what you *think* you need to your *real* need. It will pull you from seducing images, clichés, and "power statements." It will sever from you "*purposes*" that seem to give your life reason and tear away every foundation you ever laid for yourself. It will find its way into your heart and smash the idols of lust, self-indulgence, and self-esteem that you set up. It will rip apart the very fabric of your own good deeds, leaving you naked and ashamed before a holy and righteous God. This gospel is the power of God unto salvation and wherever it is preached, God saves his people.

So where do we find the gospel—the message of salvation? All the truths that are necessary to salvation are found in scripture alone. The Bible is all that we need in order to have a right relationship with God. The Bible is complete. Revelation 22:18 gives us the warning, "If any man shall add to these things, God shall add to him the plagues that are written in this book."

But is the Bible the only source of special revelation? What about what prophet so and so and what he/she said to me last week? What about the "words of knowledge" that sister so and so gave me? Aren't they from the Lord? No!

If we were to take every "revelation" that comes from pulpits today, we would have a very confused God. One says that God is doing a "new work" and that all we need are "purposes" to live by and God will give us peace and prosperity. Another says all you need to do is send in this seed offering and your miracle will be on its way. And yet another, "Just speak it into existence"—as if you are God. There is no continuity in the messages from evangelical pulpits today. Instead, we are subjected to the heresies of televangelists and false prophecies from so-called apostles and seers.

The Lord God almighty gave us his written word so that we would know what he is speaking. Hebrews 1:1 tells us that in times past he spoke through prophets and now speaks to us through his Son. That hasn't changed. In the past, before the last word of the scriptures was penned, God used prophets, kings, and even fishermen to speak his word. But now, present day, he speaks to us in his Son and that word is to be found in the Bible and nowhere else. Want to know what God is saying today? Read the Bible.

Second, the Bible is authoritative. The Old Testament writers alone make over two thousand direct claims to be speaking the very words of God. Throughout the Old Testament we read phrases such as, "The Spirit of the Lord has spoken by me," "The word of God came to me," and "Thus says the Lord." Isaiah opens his prophecy by saying, "Hear, O heavens, and give ear, O earth! For the Lord has spoken." When God speaks, everybody is to listen because he and he alone is the final authority! The Bible is not the word of man but the word of God. Although God used human agents to write scripture, 2 Timothy 3:16 tells us that all scripture is "God-breathed." Scripture is not the ideas of man but the very words of God (2 Pet 1:21). The Reformers believed, as did the earliest disciples and Church, that scripture alone was sufficient for all that we need to know God and live a godly life.

My dear friends, even if there are those who use these terms today, do not believe them. They are false prophets and imagine themselves to be something God has not called them to be. There is one single, absolute authority for the believer today, and that is the Bible. The old child's hymn says, "The B-I-B-L-E, yes that's book for me. I stand alone on the word of God, the B-I-B-L-E." Nothing has ever changed in his word, and nothing will ever change.

Third, the Bible is sufficient. Second Timothy 3:16–17 reminds us that God's word is "profitable for teaching, for reproof, for correction, for instruction in righteousness." Why? So that "the man of God may be complete, thoroughly equipped for every good work." If God's word will make us complete, why would we look to anything else? We do not need a vision, we do not need a dream, and we do not need the latest experience. What we need is a return to the sufficiency of the word of God. A marvelous picture of the absolute sufficiency of scripture is in Psalm

19:5–9. Meditate on these wonderful words. When there is a book that will transform you, make you wise, bring you joy, enlighten your eyes, endure forever, and is righteous altogether, you have no need to turn elsewhere. God's word is sufficient!

My friends, when the Holy Spirit works in our lives, it cannot be apart from his written word. The Spirit does not speak in ways that are independent of scripture. Apart from scripture we would never have known of God's grace in Christ. The biblical word, rather than spiritual experience, is the test of truth.

If we desire to see revival and reformation, it is imperative that we return to the truth of sola scriptura. The word of God is complete. The word of God is authoritative. The word of God is sufficient. The battle for the truth of God's word has been raging since the beginning of time. Satan, the great enemy of souls, began his assault with a question: "Has God said?" When many professed evangelicals are turning to the latest spiritual experiences, new moves of God, prophetic words, words of knowledge, and this idea that someone has some special anointing, we must heed Paul's command to Timothy: "Preach the word! Be ready in season and out of season. Convince, rebuke, exhort with all longsuffering and teaching" (2 Tim 4:2).

SOLA SCRIPTURA

We reaffirm the inerrant scripture to be the sole source of written divine revelation, which alone can bind the conscience. The Bible alone teaches all that is necessary for our salvation from sin and is the standard by which all Christian behavior must be measured.

We deny that any creed, council, or individual that may bind a Christian's conscience, claim that the Holy Spirit speaks independently of or contrary to what is set forth in the Bible, or claims that personal spiritual experience can ever be a vehicle of revelation.[3]

---

3. Alliance of Confessing Evangelicals, *Cambridge Declaration* [book on-line] (Alliance of Confessing Evangelicals).

3

Oops, They Did It Again!

26. *If the word of the apostles is not trustworthy, nor the scriptures which they have given us, then why is there the demand in the law for them to be accurate in their prophecies?*

27. *If today's prophets are not to be held to such great accuracy, then how can we trust the written prophetic words that are inscripturated?*

28. *The prophets and apostles have clouded their minds with visions and dreams and hidden the knowledge of the holy from their eyes so that seeing they do not see and hearing they do not hear.*

29. *Speaking forth words and prophetic utterances, being deceived themselves and blind leaders of the blind, they blaspheme the very word of God which warned that the punishments and plagues found in the Revelation of John would be upon any who added to this word, by uttering things they know nothing of.*

30. *When prophetic words are given and then do not come to pass, why are those who give them not held to account as the false prophets of the Old Testament?*

31. *"Thus saith the Lord" was also a favorite phrase of the false prophets. The only difference between those wolves in sheep's clothing in the past and those of today is the amount of media attention they receive.*

32. *A true prophet of the Lord will never give a false or "wrong" or "erred" word, as they are kept by the mighty hand of God from all error and falsehood or lies. Today's prophets feel themselves to be*

real and accurate if they can prophesy accurately only 60 percent of the time. This is anti-biblical, as scripture tells us it must be 100 percent accurate.

33. Testimonies are not proof of the word, but instead the word is to prove your testimony.

34. If we were to take every "revelation" that comes from pulpits today, we would have a very confused God. One says that God is doing a "new work" and another that we just need "purposes" to live by and God will give us peace and prosperity.

A particularly popular evangelist, with his miracle crusades, has proven himself a false prophet because he has been, rather ironically, *predictably* false with all his prophecies. Back in December 2002 he had made a prophetic "prediction" about March 3, 2003 (3/3/03). Here is part of his prophecy on December 12, 2002:

> Wednesday, the Wednesday before the twentieth would be the nineteenth, correct? No, the eighteenth of December at 2:00 a.m., I awakened to a prophecy ringing in my heart. I was hearing myself prophesy.... I will tell you this; Satan is ready to unleash horror and terror on this earth as never before. But I heard the Lord say, literally I heard him speak those words, he said, "Dark days are ahead for the world, and bright days for my people." (Applause) I was prophesying it. "Those who know me and those who walk with me will know light and beauty, says the Lord." God began to speak these words.... March third. I just heard March third in my ears. What's March third? What day is that? We do not know. I do not know what March third what day it would be? I'm not sure what I would be, I do not know what crusade or service or maybe I'm not anywhere. But I'm hearing the Lord say that to me.[1]

Since March 3, 2003, has come and gone and nothing horrific has occurred that was predicted by this charlatan, should we continue to trust anything this man says? Why should we not question everything that comes from him? Deuteronomy is clear that any "prophet" whose prophetic utterances do not come to pass should be considered a false prophet and his predictions ignored.

> Certainly it could be expected that if this kind of change (from infallible to fallible) in the nature of prophecy were to occur, a

1. Hinn, Alliance of Confessing Evangelicals, *Cambridge Declaration* [book on-line].

clear word form the Lord would forewarn God's people. Prophecy from Moses to Christ had been an embodiment of the very words of God, absolutely reliable in every syllable. If not, under the new covenant, it were to take on the form of fallible, human utterances, as this current position affirms, it might be expected that God would clearly, unequivocally indicate this drastic change in the nature of prophecy.[2]

The apostles had supreme authority, which men no longer maintain. They were infallible spokesmen for God as well as interpreters of God's word and his revelation of the Son in and through him. Their great privilege of being eyewitnesses of the Risen Savior is not something that has been maintained for all Christians, for that would mean that Christ would no longer be in heaven with the Father until that last enemy, death, is made his footstool. The apostles were directly called by God; they performed extraordinary signs, wonders, and miracles as a badge of their office. They also were able to convey those gifts to others by the laying on of hands. The gift of tongues was a gift given directly by the laying on of the hands of the apostles as well. Otherwise Peter and John would not have been needed to confer the gifts to the Samaritan believers. Also, note that Simon recognizes that the "gift" could only be conferred by the "laying on of the apostles' hands" (cf. Acts 8:18).

These modern-day apostles have no proof that they have seen the Risen Savior or have spoken God's word infallibly. Indeed, there is much proof of the exact opposite. Nor have they performed the miraculous signs and wonders that Peter, James, John, and Paul wrought in the same "on-demand" manner. Nor have they shown that they were given direct authority by God or called by Jesus personally. These men, and even, shamefully, women have taken on an office that ceased and which was not conferred to them.

There were several tests for discerning a true prophet from a false one. These tests are most imperative for our day even as it was during the time of the prophets in the land of Israel and Judah. We need to see that these tests have never changed and hold those who call themselves "prophets" to God's measuring stick to see if they measure up.

---

2. Robertson, *The Final Word: A Biblical Response to the Case for Tongues and Prophecy Today*, 97.

1. A true prophet was aware of a definite call by God to this ministry.

2. A true prophet only spoke by revelation.

3. A true prophet lived a life of holiness and awe Coram Deo (before the face of God).

4. A true prophet never prophesied for money.

5. A true prophet stood for the truth even when that meant certain death.

6. A true prophet spoke only in the name of Jehovah.

7. A true prophet's messages never contradicted previous revelations but remained in line with them. As is said now, "scripture interprets scripture," so then the words of the true prophets lined up in harmony and not in discord.

8. The prophecies of the true prophet eventually came to pass. Events in history would vindicate the prophet's ministry and confirm and authenticate his message that it was from God and not from man.

Finally, all of these criteria stand or fall upon the authority of scripture. The importance of the authority of scripture is very high because of the repercussions of views that allow discrepancies and errors and additions. Therefore, it behooves the Christian to be able to defend what the Bible says as well as Jesus's view on the inerrancy and infallibility of the texts. If a person cannot make the case for the authority of the scriptures, then he will be left to decide for himself what is true and what is false and will begin to doubt the authenticity and veracity of Jesus's testimony, life, death, and resurrection. The authority of scripture must be upheld so that any teaching that comes along the trail may be verified as authentic and biblical.

Moving on to the inspiration of the scriptures, today's prophets and apostles declare that they have received a special revelation of God or worse yet, some "divine secret" that they are going to reveal. The question here is whether they are truly speaking from God and have been given direct revelation or are self-deceived, errantly taught, deluded, or outright lying. I will give them the benefit of the doubt and say that the majority are not outright lying but have been taught wrong over previous generations. Since the mid 1840s, there has been heightened "direct revelations" from God that have made it into mainstream Christianity. Thus let us say that they are sincere.

Paul writes to Timothy in his second letter:

> All scripture is breathed out by God and profitable for teaching, for reproof, for correction, and for training in righteousness, that the man of God may be competent, equipped for every good work. (3:16–17)

In defending the inspiration of scripture, it comes down to this—in its final analysis, "Has God spoken, and has he spoken with clarity?"

> What it affirms is that the scriptures owe their origin to an activity of God the Holy Ghost and are in the highest and truest sense his creation. It is on this foundation of Divine origin that all the high attributes of scripture are built.[3]

Benjamin B. Warfield is correct when he says, "All the high attributes of scripture are built" upon this divine truth, one reflected in the views of Jesus and his apostles. Yet those who claim to be following "apostolic authority" do not follow the apostles' example in their view of scripture; and they think they know better than God when it comes to the nature of the word.

James White, in his article on theopneustos, says:

> The term, "inspiration" is a rather poor term, because it really means "God breathed" or "breathed out by God." It does not mean "breathed into" as if God raised the level of the writings of the prophets and apostles to a higher plain than that of ordinary writings of men, but it means that God actually created the scriptures and tells us that the very scriptures themselves are the creation of God, reflecting his very breath, his very speaking.[4]

Understanding that the "Thus saith the Lord" statements are created by God should give us pause when thinking we are giving out a "word from the Lord" or "word of knowledge," prophecy, or revelation. To understand the authority of the word, we must first look at the testimony of the writers. We begin with these men because they of all people should know whether the words they recorded came from themselves or from

---

3. Warfield, *Revelation and Inspiration*.
4. White, "God-Breathed; Breathed Out By God; Theopneustos."

the mind of God. Is the Bible merely a product of human creativity? That's not likely because many of the writers were unlearned men, not great classical philosophers. Some were fishermen, farmers, and tax collectors. Yet, they wrote with absolute confidence that what they recorded was the word of God. Could they have been wrong?

The Bible contains sixty-six books written by over forty authors and covers a period of at least fifteen hundred years. With only a few exceptions, the authors were Jewish men. Yet the Bible has universal appeal. Two writers were kings; two were priests; one was a physician; two were fishermen; two were shepherds. Paul was a Pharisee and a theologian; Daniel was a statesman; Matthew was a tax collector; Joshua was a soldier; Ezra was a scribe; and Nehemiah was a cupbearer. The writing of these men expanded over fifteen hundred years and yet there is not one contradiction and they develop the same perfect theme. The Bible has one doctrinal viewpoint, one moral standard, one plan of salvation, one program of the ages, and one worldview. If God did not write it, how could over forty men writing in different centuries make their thoughts harmonize? The accuracy and harmony of scriptures demand that we acknowledge their infallibility.

"THUS SAITH THE LORD" AND THE OLD TESTAMENT WRITERS

Over thirty-eight hundred times Old Testament writers claim they are writing the words of God. After giving the law, Moses said, "You shall not add to the word that I command you, nor take from it, that you may keep the commandments of the LORD your God that I command you" (Deut 4:2). Moses said:

> Now this is the commandment, the statutes and the rules that the LORD your God commanded me to teach you, that you may do them in the land to which you are going over, to possess it, that you may fear the LORD your God, you and your son and your son's son, by keeping all his statutes and his commandments, which I command you, all the days of your life, and that your days may be long. . . . And these words that I command you today shall be on your heart. You shall teach them diligently to your children, and shall talk of them when you sit in your house, and when you walk by the way, and when you lie down, and when you rise. You shall bind them as a sign on your hand, and they shall be as frontlets

between your eyes. You shall write them on the doorposts of your house and on your gates. (Deut 6:1–2, 6–9)

The words that Moses spoke were God's word directly revealed to him by the Spirit. The warnings are to be taken seriously and strictly obeyed.

"MOVED BY THE HOLY SPIRIT" AND THE NEW TESTAMENT WRITERS

New Testament writers believed the Old Testament was the word of God. Over three hundred times the New Testament directly quotes the Old. And there are over one thousand references to the Old Testament in the New.[5]

The following are examples of how the apostles viewed what they were writing. Paul's writings are referred to as scripture by Peter. The Church viewed the writings of the New Testament epistles and gospel accounts of Christ's life as authentic, direct revelation by God and they were held as infallible, inspired, and inerrant. Who today can say that about what they write or what they speak? No one.

The apostles also looked at the writings of the Old Testament as infallible, inspired, and inerrant, as directly revealed to Moses and the prophets. There was no questioning that the scriptures were God's word in the minds and hearts of the early Church.

> Second Peter 1:21 says, "Men spoke from God as they were carried along by the Holy Spirit." Peter believed the Old Testament was inspired.
>
> Romans 7:12 says, "The law is holy, and the commandment holy and righteous and good."
>
> Acts 7:37–38 says, "Moses . . . said to the Israelites, 'God will raise up for you a prophet like me from your brothers.' This is the one who was in the congregation in the wilderness with the angel who spoke to him at Mount Sinai, and with our fathers. He received living oracles to give to us." God gave his word to an angel, who gave it to a man, who gave it to us.
>
> Acts 13:34–35 says, "He [God] raised him [the Messiah] from the dead, no more to return to corruption, he has spoken in this way, 'I will give you the holy and sure blessings of David.' Therefore, he also says in another psalm, 'You will not let your Holy One see

---

5. Kaiser Jr., *The Uses of the Old Testament in the New*, 2–3.

corruption.'" In Psalm 16:10 David is speaking but here in Acts, Paul says God is the one who is speaking.

In Acts 28:25 Paul said, "Well spoke the Holy Ghost by Isaiah the prophet unto our fathers" (KJV21). Again the Holy Spirit spoke through a human instrument.

Galatians 3:8 says, "The Scripture, foreseeing that God would justify the Gentiles through faith, preached before the gospel unto Abraham saying, 'In you shall all nations be blessed.'"

The Old Testament was known to be the very word of God and the New Testament held the same lofty and special position.

THE TESTIMONY OF JESUS CHRIST

The word of God is the revelatory message given to mankind that delineates the redemptive purposes of God through the ministry of Jesus Christ, the living word. It is God's revelation to mankind of the history of redemption which is only found in completion in Jesus of Nazareth. This word of God is the only revelation whereby we are taught objective truth.

Since the theme of scripture is Jesus, it is important to learn what his view of the scriptures was. Jesus said to the Jewish leaders, "Search the Scriptures because you think that in them you have eternal life; and it is they that bear witness about me" (John 5:39). Revelation 19:10 declares, "Worship God; for the testimony of Jesus is the spirit of prophecy." "Beginning at Moses and all the Prophets, he [the Lord] interpreted to them [the disciples] in all the Scriptures, the things concerning himself" (Luke 24:27).

Jesus had a very high view of the Old Testament, referring to it on numerous occasions. He refers to events such as the Flood and Jonah as actual historical occurrences and not mythological stories. Jesus revered the Law and in fact stated that he didn't come to do away with it but to actually fulfill it.

When Jesus speaks of the creation of Adam and Eve, he is teaching about adultery and divorce. He is dealing with an actual difficulty and not some theoretical one and therefore refers to an actual historical event to teach people about marriage. With Noah and the ark, Jesus is speaking of a future historical event, his second coming, and refers to a past historical event as proof positive that judgements will occur in the future upon his return. As Jesus is teaching about his upcoming crucifixion and subsequent resurrection, he does not use an analogy from nature but refers once again to an historical event as a true event to prove that he will rise from the dead.

When Jesus was tempted by Satan, he responded each time by replying, "It is written" (Matt 4:3–10). He used the power of God's word to combat Satan.

Jesus literally fulfilled hundreds of Messianic prophecies (see Josh McDowell's *Evidence That Demands a Verdict*, 141–77). For example, Christ was born in Bethlehem (Micah 5:2; Matt 2:1), he suffered and died on a cross (Ps 22; Matt 27:46; John 19:28), and he rose from the dead (Isa 53:9–10; Ps 16:10; Matt 28).

Time and again Christ repeatedly confirmed the authority of the Old Testament. In addition, he established the sufficiency of scripture to save the elect; "They have Moses and the prophets; let them hear them" (Luke 16:29). In context his point was that miracles are not necessary for men to be saved; all that is needed is the word of the prophets.

He who is the truth knew, believed, and submitted to the inspired writings with no reservations. There are only three possibilities concerning Jesus's testimony to scripture: 1) There are no errors in scripture; 2) There are errors, but Jesus didn't know them and therefore was not God; 3) There are errors and he knew about them but covered them up and therefore he is not holy. If God is holy, then Christ is holy and then we must believe that the Bible is the word of God. There is a reason why it is called the "Holy Bible."

CONTINUED REVELATION

As for the Charismatics and their use of private revelation or contemporary prophecies, these go outside the revealed word of God and the audience has no ability to verify that it is even God speaking, let alone a foretelling of future events. Charismatic prophecies have come and gone without coming to pass and make a poor platform upon which to stand. The truncated and simplistic view that Charismatics hold to the authority of the written word of God is contradicted by the lack of validity in anything they proclaim. Revelation as we know it has ceased and therefore to use anything they might prophesy would be going outside the bounds of scripture and into error headlong.

To show you how they often speak in the first person, as if it were God himself telling us these new prophecies and revelations, I'm including an e-mail received from *Charisma Online Magazine*:

> Little by little—this is how I will advance you into the fullness of your destiny. I can reverse your losses and secure your future, but you must work with Me in new ways. I will establish your boundaries and renew your vision, but you must see as I see.
>
> I am re-knitting your emotions. Fragmentation that you have experienced in the last season should not keep you from experiencing My wholeness in your future. Do not fear, for I am proceeding and bringing you forth to a new place.
>
> The re-knitting of your emotions and realigning of your desires will set My motion in you. This will direct your feet from the wrong ways and cause you to see the pointers and signs for your right path. Do not resist the needle of mending, for I am re-knitting, finding holes and knitting again.
>
> Follow Me! For many will turn aside to seek other ways this hour. But you must follow—even if the path is rocky and steep. Do not try to keep Me from taking you to the "there" that I have prepared to give you. Also, do not try to keep Me from going to the place that I need to go to prepare the way for you.
>
> I am not like you and do not want to rest in the comfortable place that you are now occupying. Submit your emotions so I can re-knit them. You will gain new strength to resist the enemy when you submit in a new way. You are striving in areas that are not My concern. Submit, resist and then follow Me to the best that I have.[6]

Unfortunately, even among those in traditionally evangelical circles more and more believe that God is giving "new revelation." Charismatics, Pentecostals, and those in the Word of Faith or New Apostolic Reformation movements call them "revelation knowledge." They look at their dreams and say God is speaking to them. Or they imagine they hear voices and it is God speaking. But let's see the reason for revelation.

Natural revelation tells us that there is a Creator. Then patriarchal revelation, by dreams, visions, and voices, told us the lineage and covenant of the Messiah. The Mosaic revelation, in the law given and written, told us what was expected of us and was to be a tutor for us to come and recognize our need of a Savior. The prophetic revelation came to explain

---

6. Charisma, e-mail message to nancy@silentcryministries.org, August 14, 2007.

the law and give clearer understanding and revelations of Christ; but the apostolic revelations completed, fulfilled, and explained all that was threatened, promised, and taught. Now, we must expect no new revelation but only more of the Spirit of Christ to help us better understand what is already revealed. The Spirit no longer reveals "words from God" but rather illuminates the word already given.

The primary reason for all revelation was to point to Jesus Christ the Savior and Redeemer of God's people. Practically speaking, since Christ has come, and he was the primary reason for revelation, there is *no need* any longer for revelation. Paul spoke of the "mystery," which was the coming of Christ and the inclusion of the elect Gentiles in the plan of salvation. Since Jesus has come, died, and risen again, and his story is given in the gospels, the message of salvation has been fully revealed. What need is there for further revelation?

Peter says that revelation was not for personal interpretation, nor for personal direction. All revelation pointed to one who was to come and be the propitiation for the sins of God's people. Having completed that task, there is no longer a need to tell of what he will come to do, but what he has done has been faithfully and inerrantly written down for each succeeding generation.

The supremacy of the gospel revelation, which God spoke through his Son, is far above all those who came previously. Simeon, the priest at the circumcision of Jesus, called him "a light for revelation to the Gentiles." Paul says that he received the gospel by direct revelation of Jesus Christ (Gal 1:12). Jesus is the final, finishing revelation. Jesus is "the final word." He is the most direct revelation we will ever have, and he is the ultimate revelation.

Those who think we still need revelation today do nothing but spit upon Christ as if he is not sufficient. The beauty of the revelation through Christ is that everything from the first revelation about the one who was to come and crush the serpent's head is in total agreement with the last prophecy in Malachi that he will send his messenger before the Messiah/Servant. Nothing is contradictory with the prophetic utterances in the scriptures.

However, today on TV or on Christian radio we hear such phrases as, "I had a revelation . . ." "I had this vision . . ." or "God spoke to me and revealed . . ." When we listen to what God has revealed to these supposed and false prophets, and if we are to compare them, we will come away with a God who is no God because he's telling people contradictory things.

Scripture tells us in Hebrews 1:2 that God has spoken to us in his Son ... There is a sense of culmination. This final word is at its pinnacle. This is the height, the peak of what God has been revealing for four thousand years up to this point. It's like the capstone being placed on the building. There is a sense of it being the end, of prophetic words being terminated. This is not because God doesn't speak but because his final word is in his Son, Jesus our Lord and Savior, and now he speaks through his Son, who is found in the written word.

There is no greater final authority, no more direct word, and no more accurate revelation than what we have been given in the scriptures. And we know that Paul said to the Corinthians that we know in part, we prophesy in part, and when that which is "complete" comes, the full revelation of the message of Jesus Christ (what we call that the New Testament), then prophecies will stop. But why did they stop? They stopped because Jesus is the final word. He is the final revelation from God with regard to our salvation—the way to everlasting life and redemption.

But is the Bible the only source of special revelation? What about what prophet so and so and what he/she said to me last week? What about the "words of knowledge" that sister so and so gave me? Aren't they from the Lord? No!

The Lord God almighty gave us his written word so that we would know what he is speaking—so that we wouldn't wonder what his will is for us. He gave us his word so that we wouldn't walk around not knowing what he expects of us and what he plans for us. We show absolute disrespect for God by not reading his word but instead leaving it on the shelf until Sunday or Bible study. In fact, I was at a women's gathering where the speaker asked us to pick up our Bibles. We all did. Her response was, "Well ladies you won't need that (*your Bible*) today so put it under your chair" (italics mine). Unfortunately, I was too young in the Lord to understand that everything we need for life and godliness we already have revealed to us, objectively and infallibly, in the scriptures. We are privileged people because we have God's final word and we dishonor him by *neglecting it so often*.

There is another aspect to look into with regard to the office of prophet. A prophet stood between God and man in a position of mediator. The prophet was there to speak forth God's word to God's people so that they knew what was required of them, whether there was sin "in the camp," and what the people were to do. The office of prophet carried with it the weight of the very voice of God and they could not ever be wrong. The office also foreshadowed the prophet who was to come in the similitude of Moses. Now that the prophet has come, and the word of God has been revealed, there is no need for another mediator because Jesus is the one mediator between God and man.

Men would seek out prophets because they could not, prior to Christ's coming, hear a word from the Lord apart from one. As O. Palmer Robertson states in his book *The Final Word*, "The ultimate goal of God's covenant cannot be realised so long as a prophetic figure must stand between the Lord and his people."[7] The teaching that prophets and apostles still function within the Church forces her people to run to them to "hear the word of the Lord" when they should be directed not to men or women but to God's only sure source for his word, the scriptures.

The second effect of such ideas is that they make first- and second-class of citizens within the Kingdom of God. The first class are those with a greater anointing. They hear the voice of God, speak directly to him, and receive direct revelation for others. They position themselves between God and man as mediators usurping the rightful place that belongs solely to Jesus Christ of Nazareth. The second class then are forced to go "up to the front" to be given personal prophecies or words of knowledge and revelation understanding so that they know whether to marry this one or that, what school to attend, where to buy dinner, and other such nonsense. The result of this reduces the sacred word to a magic "eight ball" for believers to discern what move they are to make next in their lives. The people of God are forced into witchcraft and willingly follow the "anointed prophet" down the cliff into heresy and destruction.

However, as long as these prophets and apostles run up the mountain and back down to the people below to bring them some new revelation knowledge or understanding, God's covenantal unity will never be enjoyed. The presence of a mediator directly suggests that there is still a separation between God and his people, between their Father and his children. Yet God himself has come down as the final prophet and mediator and the covenantal unity is fulfilled, thereby ending the intermediary work of the prophetic figure. With finality, God has now spoken to

---

7. Robertson, *The Final Word: A Biblical Response to the Case for Tongues and Prophecy Today*, 4.

us through his Son, Jesus Christ, ending the need for a mediator only foreshadowed by the prophets both under the Old Testament era and the New. No longer is a go-between needed, for there is "one Mediator between God and man, the Man Jesus Christ" (1 Tim 2:5).

Previously, we looked at the importance of accuracy, inerrancy, and infallibility when it comes to revelations from God. The Bible lays a heavy weight upon those who "speak for God" or have "prophetic utterances" or "revelatory knowledge." The penalty for false prophets was serious, severe, and swift. It was serious because the man or woman was lying and therefore deceiving the people of God, whether the Old Testament Church (Israel) or the Jewish/Gentile/Global Church of the New Testament. It was severe because it called for the death penalty. It was swift because God would not allow lies to continue in his covenantal people. God wanted to speak to his people, and he would not allow falsehood to be spoken in his name.

The test for a false prophet is rather simple: if it comes to pass, it is from God. If the prophet is wrong once, though he may prophesy 99 percent of the time correctly, the man or woman is a false prophet.

WHAT WERE THE SCRIPTURAL TESTS FOR A PROPHET? HOW WERE THEY VALIDATED?

How do we know if a person claiming to give revelation from God is a true prophet? Fortunately, the scripture gives us several tests and tells us to test the prophets by them (cf. 1 John 4:1; Matt 7:15–20):

- Do they utter false prophecies (Deut 18:21–22)?

  "And if you say in your heart, 'How may we know the word that the LORD has not spoken?'—when a prophet speaks in the name of the LORD, if the word does not come to pass or come true, that is a word that the LORD has not spoken; the prophet has spoken it presumptuously. You need not be afraid of him."

- Do they preach another gospel (Gal 1:8)?

  "But even if we or an angel from heaven should preach to you a gospel contrary to the one we preached to you, let him be accursed."

- Do they follow another God (Deut 13:1–2)?

    "If a prophet or a dreamer of dreams arises among you and gives you a sign or a wonder, and the sign or wonder that he tells you comes to pass, and if he says, 'Let us go after other gods,' which you have not known, 'and let us serve them.'"

- Is the focus of their prophecies apart from Christ (Rev 19:10)?

    "Then I fell down at his feet to worship him, but he said to me, 'You must not do that! I am a fellow servant with you and your brothers who hold to the testimony of Jesus. Worship God.' For the testimony of Jesus is the spirit of prophecy."

- Do they deny that Jesus is Lord (1 Cor 12:3)?

    "Therefore I want you to understand that no one speaking in the Spirit of God ever says 'Jesus is accursed!' and no one can say 'Jesus is Lord' except in the Holy Spirit."

- Do they have new revelation since the time of the apostles (Heb 1:1; 2:3–4; John 14:26; John 16:13; Acts 1:21–22)?

    Long ago, at many times and in many ways, God spoke to our fathers by the prophets. (Heb 1:1)

    How shall we escape if we neglect such a great salvation? It was declared at first by the Lord, and it was attested to us by those who heard, while God also bore witness by signs and wonders and various miracles and by gifts of the Holy Spirit distributed according to his will. (Heb 2:3–4)

    But the helper, the Holy Spirit, whom the Father will send in my name, he will teach you all things and bring to your remembrance all that I have said to you. (John 14:26)

    When the Spirit of truth comes, he will guide you into all the truth, for he will not speak on his own authority, but whatever he hears he will speak, and he will declare to you the things that are to come. (John 16:13)

    So one of the men who have accompanied us during all the time that the Lord Jesus went in and out among us, beginning from the baptism of John until the day when he was taken up from us—one of these men must become with us a witness to his resurrection. (Acts 1:21–22)

It is important to note that each of these is a disqualifier. If any one single point is maintained by the person, we can be sure that we do not have a true prophet. The final test makes for testing prophets now easier than in the early stage of the Church age.

Beyond these negative tests, there is a positive test; miracles. People who gave revelation from God were associated with supernatural activity, either through them or associated with them. Miracles were performed in order to authenticate the message being delivered by God's servant as being revelation from God, without error:

- Christ's works validated his message (Acts 2:22; cf. John 10:24–26; 11:47–48; 20:30–31).

    Men of Israel, hear these words: Jesus of Nazareth, a man attested to you by God with mighty works and wonders and signs that God did through him in your midst, as you yourselves know—this Jesus, delivered up according to the definite plan and foreknowledge of God, you crucified and killed by the hands of lawless men. (Acts 2:22-23)

    So the Jews gathered around him and said to him, "How long will you keep us in suspense? If you are the Christ, tell us plainly." Jesus answered them, "I told you, and you do not believe. The works that I do in my Father's name bear witness about me, but you do not believe because you are not part of my flock." (John 10:24-26)

    So the chief priests and the Pharisees gathered the Council and said, "What are we to do? For this man performs many signs. If we let him go on like this, everyone will believe in him, and the Romans will come and take away both our place and our nation." (John 11:47-48)

    Now Jesus did many other signs in the presence of the disciples, which are not written in this book; but these are written so that you may believe that Jesus is the Christ, the Son of God, and that by believing you may have life in his name. (John 20:30-31)

- The apostles' miracles were signs to authenticate their message (2 Cor 12:12; Rom 15:18–20; Heb 2:3–4; cf. Acts 2:43; 5:12).

    The signs of a true apostle were performed among you with utmost patience, with signs and wonders and mighty works. (2 Cor 2:12)

> For I will not venture to speak of anything except what Christ has accomplished through me to bring the Gentiles to obedience—by word and deed, by the power of signs and wonders, by the power of the Spirit of God—so that from Jerusalem and all the way around to Illyricum I have fulfilled the ministry of the gospel of Christ; and thus I make it my ambition to preach the gospel, not where Christ has already been named, lest I build on someone else's foundation. (Rom 15:18–20)

> How shall we escape if we neglect such a great salvation? It was declared at first by the Lord, and it was attested to us by those who heard, while God also bore witness by signs and wonders and various miracles and by gifts of the Holy Spirit distributed according to his will. (Heb 2:3–4)

> And awe came upon every soul, and many wonders and signs were being done through the apostles. (Acts 2:43)

> Now many signs and wonders were regularly done among the people by the hands of the apostles. And they were all together in Solomon's Portico. (Acts 5:12)

- Moses's miracles confirmed for Israel and for Pharaoh that he was divinely appointed.
- Elijah's miracles validated the words that he spoke as being from the Lord.

> And the woman said to Elijah, "Now I know that you are a man of God, and that the word of the LORD in your mouth is truth." (1 Kgs 17:24)

Miracles were signs and seals of the ministry of the apostles. These were not the type we hear about today, which are miracles that cannot be medically verified or even seen with the eye. Attend a conference or crusade with one of these prophets or apostles headlining and the type of miracles we are given are of the type that cannot be verified on the spot. Often the miracle will have something to do with pain or aggravation within the body of the person. But the type witnessed to in the scriptures—lame men leaping, deaf men hearing perfectly, tongues loosed completely, and dead men raised instantaneously—these you will not see. The apostles were able to authenticate their office with what might be termed "miracles on demand." Wherever they went, the sick were healed, but always as testimony to the power and authenticity of the message of the resurrection. These were not showmen who put on a good act with lights and sound and proper introductory music as one "prophet" does at his every crusade. No, these were men of God who preached the gospel of grace and the resurrection of Jesus who had this testimony authenticated until the completion of the message in written form.

But with regard to the false prophecies of these apostles and prophets, we must not forget that both Old and New Testament prophets were held to an accuracy rating of 100 percent with every word they spoke where they were declaring it to be direct revelation from the Lord. If they faulted once, just one single time, the people of God were to relegate them to the false prophet category and never worry again about their campfire tales. With regard to the passage in Deuteronomy 18:22, Matthew Henry writes:

> Since it is so great a duty to hearken to the true prophets, and yet there is so much danger of being misled by false prophets, *how shall we know the word which the Lord has not spoken?* By what marks may we discover a cheat? Note, It highly concerns us to have a right touchstone wherewith to try the word we hear, that we may know what that word is which the Lord has not spoken. Whatever is directly repugnant to sense, to the light and law of nature, and to the plain meaning of the written word, we may be sure is not that which the Lord has spoken; nor that which gives countenance and encouragement to sin, or has a manifest tendency to the destruction of piety or charity: far be it from God that he should contradict himself. The rule here given in answer to this enquiry was adapted chiefly to that state, Deuteronomy 18:22. If there was any cause to suspect the sincerity of a prophet, let them observe that if he gave them any sign, or foretold something to come, and the event was not according to his prediction, they might be sure he was not sent of God. This does not refer so much to the foretelling of mercies and judgments (though as to these, and the difference between the predictions of mercies and judgments, there is a rule of discerning between truth and falsehood laid down by the prophet, Jeremiah 28:8–9), but rather to the giving of signs on purpose to confirm their mission. Though the sign did come to pass, yet this would not serve to prove their mission if they called them to serve other Gods; this point had been already settled, Deuteronomy 13:1–3.

But, if the sign did not come to pass, this would serve to disprove their mission.[8]

The test is simple: if the sign to confirm the word does not come to pass, the person is a false prophet and they are not to fear the person, but instead should fear God that they followed such a rogue.

Well, let us take some of the recent prophecies from several so-called prophets and apostles and test them to see if what they prophesied did indeed come to pass.

I have chosen not to name anyone within the pages of this book but only to index them and reference them in the bibliography at the end of this work. This I have chosen so that you do not become distracted by the person but instead pay close attention to the facts.

A "woman apostle and prophetess" at a women's conference in California in 1996 called "Women of the Word" said that *"the divorce rate for Christians would be cut in half within one year."*[9]

> And now in the year 2000 *we're trying to establish the prophetic and apostolic around the world.* And I'm telling you God is moving all over the world. There is a hunger in every nation for the prophets and the apostles. Because God's stirring it up. And in this book I tell you about three more major moves of God that must take place before the second coming of Jesus transpires. And we're, and we're, how God's restored all fivefold ministry to get the saints ready for the saints' movement.[10]

The gifts and offices of the Spirit have always been active in the Church, though we no longer have foundational apostles and prophets as these men and women claim they are. God does not need to reinstate something that he already has, and doesn't need the New Apostolic Reformation (NAR) to "establish the prophetic and apostolic around the world." What this man is talking about is "re-instating" something unbiblical.

> You see I prophesy over you a new dimension, and I just speak by the Spirit of God and the Lord said I'm raising up a new leadership

---

8. Henry, *A Commentary on the Holy Bible*, 6 vols.

9. Jacobs, "National School of the Prophets—Mobilizing the Prophetic Office," Brochure for Colorado Springs Conference.

10. Hamon, *National School of the Prophets—Mobilizing the Prophetic Office*, (Session 11).

in the earth and the Lord said "Truly there is a leader shift taking place and I'm moving my leaders into new positions and into new anointings."[11]

There is only one anointing (cf. 1 John 2:27) and there are no new gifts of the Spirit that are different from anything that has gone before. Worse than this, another "apostle" claims God is moving us into a "new grace."

> And the Lord says *"I'm giving you new grace* to begin to operate and function apostolically and prophetically like you've never known before and there is anew dimension of my grace and my glory that's even being released upon my leaders in this hour and you shall rise up with a new force and with a new authority and with a new power and with a new strength and with a new dynamic in your churches and you shall begin to see breakthroughs that you've never seen before," says the Lord, "For I break off the limitations that have tried to hold you back and have tried to hold back your gift and have tried to hold back your church, I begin to break the limitations through apostolic and prophetic release," *so the Lord said. "Get ready, I'm shifting you, I'm moving you into a new grace.* For all over the earth there is a new breed being raised up. There was a new leadership coming into place and many men and women are taking their place in leadership and *the apostles are rising and the prophets are rising and even the elders of the local churches are rising into a new dimension of grace* to begin to release that which is not been released in generations."[12]
>
> So the Lord says, "Do not draw back but press into this dimension, for it is a new dimension for my leaders," and the Lord said, "And each city and each region *a new breed of prophetic and apostolic leaders shall be raised up and you shall begin to do what you could not do before and you shall begin to release my grace and my anointing upon the people.*"[13]

Jesus Christ is the author and giver of grace and the anointing that is his alone. This sounds similar to the Romanist doctrine where they claim Mary releases the grace of God to people. The new apostles and prophets actually believe that they are the ones who can impart grace and gifts to people. They had better humble themselves before God and realize they are just unworthy, sinful, and rebellious.

11. Eckhardt, "Mobilizing the Prophetic Office."
12. Ibid.
13. Ibid.

Oops, They Did It Again!

One who claims to be the leading apostle and prophet of Church history endorses a number of false prophesies made by his prophets, even though he claims to be a "horizontal apostle" who brings all the ministries in the body of Christ together.[14]

In the book *Breaking Strongholds in Your City,* the author claims:

> "Ten million Japanese will come to Christ by the year 2000." He also claims his spiritual warfare techniques "Deposed dictator Manual Noriega, lowered the crime rate in Los Angeles, and broke the power of demons over Japan."[15]

> There will be a persecution of the Jews in Russia that will notably escalate during the fall of 2000.[16]

Yet another prophet says:

> I had a dream in which Billy Graham was talking to me about his crusade in New York in 1957. A crusade that lasted 3 1/2 months, 2,000,000 people came through the doors of Madison Square Garden, and 55,000 people were saved. As I listened to Billy Graham speak in my dream, my heart just broke for New York City, I started weeping I wept so hard that when I woke up, my pillow was soaked with tears. As I got out of bed, I knew we have to go to New York and launch one of the biggest soul winning crusades since 1957. It just dropped in my spirit and I knew it by the Holy Ghost.[17]

So the pastor they call the "Holy Ghost Bartender" promised that thousands were going to come and 150,000 people were going to be saved. He states this as a matter of fact because the Holy Spirit dropped it in "his spirit." This is a claim to a direct revelation from God. Well, let's see what happened.

This article is from *Christian News Today*:

> The Tampa Tribune reported that South African Evangelist's *(name withheld)* New York Crusade is a flop. Rodney taught pastors that "sheep needed to be fleeced or they would have too much hair and

---

14. Wagner, "Mobilizing the Pophetic Office," *National School of the prophets*, Session 1.

15. Wagner, *Breaking Strongholds in Your City: How to Use Spiritual Mapping to Make Your Prayers More Strategic, Effective, and Targeted*, 25.

16. Simpson, "Deception in the Church," (accessed July 15, 2007).

17. Brown, and Rodney, "Rodney Browne comes to NY," 1997.

could not see where they are going. It was the pastor's job to fleece the sheep."

NEW YORK—You know what they say about New York: If you can make it here, you can make it anywhere. That said, Tampa evangelist *(name withheld)*, in the final days of his multimillion-dollar, six week crusade in Madison Square Garden, is scaling down his plans for next summer. "We're going to Shreveport," he says.

The mainly black and Hispanic crowds average about 3,000 a night in the famed 19,000 seat arena. Even though the free meetings include entertainment, *(name withheld)* "Good News New York" campaign has failed to attract the size audience he wanted.

They did not even come for Carman, the popular Christian singer from neighbouring New Jersey who drew more than 25,000 fans to a 1996 concert at Tropicana Field in St. Petersburg. Only 5,600 showed up for his 40 minute music set Saturday. "New York's a hard place, even when you have support," says the Rev. David Epstein, pastor of Calvary Baptist Church in Manhattan.

(Name withheld) his goal was to "shake the Big Apple to its core" by sharing the good news of the Gospel of Jesus Christ. But he's had many obstacles along the way: a blistering heat wave, New York's obsession with the sudden death of John F. Kennedy Jr. and his association with the controversial "holy laughter" movement.

That movement is how *(name withheld)*, known as the "Holy Ghost bartender," made his reputation. At services in the Tampa area and around the world, followers are overcome with the Holy Spirit and laugh uncontrollably.

(Name withheld) stuck to his promise to keep the crusade strictly evangelical. However, that may have contributed to the low attendance. "*(Name withheld)* coming into the Garden without holy laughter is like David Copperfield putting on a show without magic tricks," said one New York writer.[18]

Let's look at some other prophetic utterances:

"1950s *(name withheld)* was believed him to be the prophet Elijah who was to come before the return of Christ Jesus. I sincerely believe and maintain as a private student of the word along with Divine Inspiration that 1977 ought to terminate the world systems and usher in the Millennium" (*Seven Church Ages*, 322). Branham proclaimed himself the angel of Revelation 3:14 and 10:7 and prophesied that by 1977 all denominations would be consumed by

---

18. "Good News America is a Flop! No Signs or Wonders!" *Christian News Today*, 1999.

Oops, They Did It Again!

the World Council of Churches under the control of the Roman Catholics, that the Rapture would take place, and that the world would be destroyed (*Dictionary of Pentecostal and Charismatic Movements*, 96).[19]

(*Name withheld*) in his book *I Predict 2000 A.D.* said, "I predict the absolute fullness of mans operation on planet earth by the year 2,000 AD. Then Jesus Christ shall reign from Jerusalem for 1,000 years."[20]

June 9, 1994, was the most recent big blunder of many. It was predicted that evil would be ripped from the world on June 9 on TBN; everyone was excited. It would be the most cataclysmic event since the resurrection. It would be the day of the Lord (the tribulation?) or the day the son of man as revealed. Using Isaiah 25:6–9, which is the reference for the literal coming of Christ, (*name withheld*) said, "I was awakened and the Lord spoke to me in the most awesome voice. I heard it outside and inside and as I sat up he said on Thursday June the ninth, I will rip the evil out of this world."[21]

Many others received the same type of message.

This is a cleansing that removes evil from the whole world and activates a worldwide spiritual revival with millions of people pouring into the church.[22]

2000 (*name withheld*)—On his television broadcast, he declared: "The Bible teaches that an antichrist comes to power (Rev. 13:1)—a world dictator... This world dictator could appear anywhere from now to 2003 (July 2, 1997)."

On his website the author once promoted his book *On the Edge of Eternity* in which he predicted that the year 2001 would "usher in international chaos such as we've never seen in our history."[23] This supposed prophet predicted this event in 2001, would:

Afflict entire populations throughout the [African] continent ... By the year 2001, there will be global chaos." He also stated,

---

19. Brenham.
20. Sumerall.
21. Hinckel.
22. Hackman, *The Evangelist*.
23. Van Impe, "quoting from *On the Edge of Eternity*," Religious Tolerance.org, (accessed August 6, 2007).

A Modern Ninety-Five

> "Widespread religious deception will be commonplace, leading to the dawn of a virtually unopposed one-world church controlled by demonic hosts (Rev. 9:20). *Christians, beware of the seductive spirits that will soon descend on all our houses (1 Tim 4:11)* . . . Ezekiel 38 predicts what is *now taking place* . . . and much more. (Likely if Y2K is as a bad as some *predict?*)[24]

However, we know now, having passed Y2K, that absolutely nothing horrific or even minor occurred.

The problem here is not that there are false prophets, because we know there will always be someone trying to direct us away from the Lord. The serious problem here is, however, that no matter how many times Charismatic televangelists make outlandish false "prophecies," they keep right on claiming the Lord has spoken directly to them, and people keep right on following them. What concerns me is the lack of accountability by these pastors, preachers, laymen, prophets, and apostles to recognize that they have been wrong on more than one occasion and that biblically, one wrong prophecy declares them false prophets.

To show how unbridled these men and women are about claiming direct revelation from God, let us read some recent prophecies while noticing that none of them came to pass. A televangelist mega-preacher used a false prophecy to extort money from the television audience and those in attendance. Declaring the following, he brought in hundreds of thousands of dollars. The question should be asked, "Since the prophecies did not come to pass, shouldn't the televangelist have sent back the money?"

> The year 1999 will be a year of plenty and the year 2000 would bring disaster.

The prophecy continued that if the audience did not double their donations in 1999, they would not survive the disaster in 2000. Those who had already made pledges were told they must call back and double their pledge.

Now that we are past the years 1999 and 2000, we know for a fact that 1999 was not a year of plenty, neither the year 2000 a year of disasters. Who knows how many were bilked out of possibly millions of dollars by taking heed to the warnings of this false prophet. Yet he continues to

---

24. Van Impe (7/1/1997).

claim that he receives direct revelations from God and is God's mouthpiece on earth today.

Another false prophecy from this same person is the following:

> The Lord also tells me to tell you in mid 90s—about '94 or '95, no later than that—God will destroy the homosexual community of America...he will destroy it with fire.[25]

It is hard to believe that God cannot make up his mind as to what year to destroy the homosexual community. Not that God will do that specifically as opposed to destroying murderers, liars, thieves, and the like separate from any other group. That will come on judgment day, and we need to pray for every sinner no matter the sin that binds them. So, in this particular prophecy, God could not decide whether it would occur in 1994 or 1995. Since when did God guess about when he would bring something to pass?

It occurred to me while writing this that Charismatics have a type of god that open theism teaches, one who does not know for certain what will occur or when it will occur. Their prophecies are never fulfilled and their reasoning is that man was able to thwart the purpose or judgment of God by giving donations.

Open theists deny that God knows the future exhaustively. In their view, God is often ignorant about what will happen,[26] a) sometimes even mistaken.[27] b) He "expresses frustration"[28] c) when people do things he had not anticipated. He changes his mind when things don't go as he had hoped.[29] d) In these contentions, open theists admittedly differ from "the classical view of God worked out in the western tradition"[30] e) that prevailed from the early Church Fathers to the present with a few exceptions. This classical view has been the position of all Christian theological traditions: Eastern Orthodox, Roman Catholic, and all forms of Protestantism. It affirms that God has complete knowledge of everything that happens in the past, present, and future. Thus open theism denies the historic

---

25. Alnor, "Benny Hinn—False Prophet Extraordinaire," (accessed August 10, 2007).

26. Pinnock et al, *The Openness of God: A Biblical Challenge to the Traditional Understanding of God,* 121–24.

27. Sanders, *The God Who Risks: A Theology of Divine Providence,* 132–33.

28. Ibid.

29. Ibid.

30. Ibid.

Christian view of God's omniscience. The present article will discuss the major issues in the controversy between the classical view and the open view. Their prophecies are never fulfilled and their reasoning is that man was able to thwart the purpose or judgment of God by giving donations.

Here are just a few more from several different prophets and apostles:

> The Spirit of God tells me—an earthquake will hit the east coast of America and destroy much in the 90s.[31]

> The Spirit tells me—Fidel Castro will die in the 90s... Holy Spirit just said to me it'll be worse than any death you can imagine.[32]

> Get ready, for there shall be a creation of a computer that shall supersede everything that has been invented up to this point. It shall be so rapid, and there shall be no more viruses that shall come and be able to touch your systems.[33]

> Under the anointing, Miss (*Name withheld*) said the day will come when the anointing of God will so increase upon his Church that every sick believer will be healed by the power of almighty God. There will not be one sick Christian![34]

> God wants us to go to the back streets. He wants to have a cure for AIDS. He said it's going to be by the year 2002, there's going to be a cure for AIDS. Well, somebody said, "Well, those homosexuals deserve to have AIDS." No they do not. You deserve to die, but Jesus died for you 2,000 years ago. I do not think anybody deserves to die. There's gonna be a cure and there's gonna be a Christian that is a scientist that's gonna come across a discovery.[35]

These so-called prophets and apostles knowingly promote the false prophecies of their compatriots and though knowing that they are false or straight-out lies, they continue to put them forth as if they are true. For this example I have left the names of the guilty in place so that you may be warned and aware and run from these dangerous wolves and heretics.

In 1983 a major apostle in the movement made a "prophecy" that there would be three months of drought. His partner said at the time:

---

31. Hinn.
32. Alnor, "The Alnor Report," 1/33/01.
33. Clement.
34. Hinn, *Honolulu Blaisdale Crusade*, January 21, 1999.
35. Clement (*Praise the Lord* TBN 12/26/2000).

> Kansas City was known as the bread-basket of the world; it was the centre of grain farming, fanning out to a radius of five hundred miles. For the whole of June there was no rain! It was terrible! For the whole of July there was no rain! It was terrible! No rain during the first week of August or the second or the third. It was terrible! Bob Jones said that the Lord had told him it would come on 23rd August. We had all been poised since early dawn that day, but by 1 pm there was still no rain. By six o'clock we were just resigned to wait another day when suddenly it began. And did it rain? It poured! No man could have manipulated that. It just had to be God![36]

Pretty impressive, isn't it? However, since the Bible tells us to prove everything ("But test everything; hold fast what is good [cf. 1 Thess 5:21].), then maybe we should take a look at the alleged accuracy of the prophecy.

A pastor of a Charismatic church in Kansas City discovered that the whole prophecy was a lie! He acknowledged that there was no drought! The U.S. National Weather Bureau confirmed that seven inches of rain fell on Kansas City in June 1983. It rained on twelve out of thirty days—almost half the month!

> On just one of those days, the rainfall was seven times the rainfall on 23rd August! So, the prophecy was a lie and a fake. What is far worse, is that the partner in prophecy, afterward (that is, after knowing what really happened, and after knowing the prophecy to be false) claimed it to be true! But, even if the prediction had turned out to be completely accurate, it had no relevance whatever for either the local church or for the universal Church.[37]

It behooves us to call these men and women to task and recognize that they have been speaking lies and deceiving, if possible, even the elect. The Church must rise up and hold these people accountable and if they remain unrepentant, they must be disciplined by being banned from the Lord's Supper and fellowship with the saints and if still unrepentant, excommunicated. But it cannot stop there. The Church must publicly acknowledge their false prophesies and warn others against going to their churches, meetings, crusades, and "miracle explosion revivals."

---

36. Ibid.
37. Napier, "The Kansas City Prophets," (accessed July 16, 2007).

A Modern Ninety-Five

This is not the only time these apostles and prophets have been caught in outright deception. In a *World Harvest Interview*, the owner/operator was sharing how "spiritual mapping" and other cultic practices had direct impact on "power evangelism." According to this interview (which can be seen on the Apologetics Coordination Team's *New Apostolic Reformation* DVDs[38]), he shares how 21 million people were praying for India in October 1993. There was a celebration for one of the many gods of India and suddenly there was an earthquake that shook the town where this celebration was occurring. The difficulty with this story lies not in the possibility of it occurring, but in the fact that it did not occur.

In researching this "testimony," which is supposed to prove the validity of heretical teaching such as prayer walking, spiritual mapping, etc., I visited the United States Geological Society's website to verify if there had indeed been an earthquake in India in October 1993. According to their records[39] (see link in bibliography), the only earthquake that hit India was in September. Now, if the people were praying in October and C. Peter Wagner states the earthquake hit in October, why is there no record of such a quake? According to Wagner, this became so well known that it boosted the teaching of "spiritual mapping" and "prayer walking." This could well be placed next to all the "fish stories" people tell to bolster their position in others' eyes, but it is a lie and purposeful deception.

Scripture tells us that we are to "contend for the faith that was once for all delivered to the saints" (Jude 1:3). Somehow, the Church of the past two centuries has *failed* that task and allowed errors and heresies of every type into the hallowed halls of our churches, damaging countless lives with false and abhorrent teachings and lies packaged in "prophetic words."

However, the prophets and apostles do not want to be accountable. In fact, they teach opposite of the scriptures with regard to proving and discerning prophecies and the spirit.

> Do not be critical. Do not be critical of it. You say, "The Bible says to be critical of prophesying." No it doesn't. You read 1 Thessalonians 5. It says, "... quench not the spirit, despise not prophesying, prove all things." You know what some critics say? Prove prophecy and be crucial and analytical. There's not one scripture that says you just sit out there where they are critical, condemning, suspicious,

---

38. Freed, "New Apostolic Reformation," (accessed July 20, 2007).
39. "United States Geological Society," (accessed July 17, 2007).

antagonistic, and negative attitude while they're prophesying. I'm going to judge it. You're unscriptural. Now you're to check out everything. "Prove all things." It did not say prove all prophecies.[40]

But, again, it must be asked, "What does scripture say about testing the spirits? About judging? Implementing discernment?"

Many years ago, my husband and I were caught up in neo-Montanism. Montanism was a group in the post-Apostolic Church that believed in ongoing revelation, of the continuation of prophetic utterances, visions, dreams, and prophets. Neo-Montanism is the modern version, which has an unbalanced view of eschatology or the end times, focusing on the immanency of the second coming to the point where they leave off their earthly responsibilities and wait idly for the second coming. They believe that women should be ordained and in roles of authority over men, and they have an unwillingness to submit to other recognized Church authorities including the writings and teachings of the past centuries of Christianity.

Each year my husband and I would attend a Christian retreat where we would sit under the teachings of these neo-Montanists and receive our "fresh anointing" in order to have the power to declare "God's Kingdom" over all the influential places. We were taught that our words were powerful and that to fully understand how God was moving us in the realm of possibility, we needed to have further revelations directly from God. We were told that we have to see "the stuff, the power, the miracles" in order for the unsaved to get curious and "choose Jesus." Without the signs and wonders, it was explained, no one would ever come to Jesus. I guess they had forgotten about the past two thousand years since the apostles' day when signs and wonders were no longer necessary.

At the time of writing this chapter, my husband and I are once again attending this camp. However, the reason we attend now is to enable people attending to discuss what is being taught and to show them what the scriptures say about the teachings while we trust the Lord to graciously extend his hand of mercy upon them and show them the error and heretical teachings this movement espouses. It is at these meetings that we are warned not to judge and "Get rid of your theology" in order to "get stupid for Jesus." Discernment is taught to be judging in a harsh way and no one should ever judge because "that's God's job . . . not ours, ever." This attitude

---

40. Hammon, "National School of the Prophets," 5/11/2000.

forgets that scripture says we are to "judge rightly" (cf. John 7:24) and "test everything" (cf. 1 Thess 5:21) while specifically "testing the spirits" (cf. 1 John 4:1) to see whether or not they are of God. However, these leaders seem to recognize that if people actually begin to study the word, they will see the error of the teaching. Instead of studying the word, they are told to "get stupid for Jesus" and just "trust the flow of the spirit" (whatever spirit that might be—it's not the Holy Spirit). They admonish us to not worry about the oddities but just go with the flow.

During our time at the retreat, we recognized many scriptures either taken out of context to appeal to the message or twisted, and in one case actually changed (i.e., the parable of the sower and the seed. We were told that the "seed" is the Kingdom while the Bible tells us, in Jesus's own words, that the "seed" is the word of God.). We were told that the "prophets were all wealthy" and that God doesn't want us poor. This is what scripture says about the prophets of old:

> Some were tortured, refusing to accept release, so that they might rise again to a better life. Others suffered mocking and flogging, and even chains and imprisonment. They were stoned, they were sawn in two, they were killed with the sword. They went about in skins of sheep and goats, destitute, afflicted, mistreated—of whom the world was not worthy—wandering about in deserts and mountains, and in dens and caves of the earth. And all these, though commended through their faith, did not receive what was promised, since God had provided something better for us, that apart from us they should not be made perfect. (Heb 11:35–40)

As for the Charismatics and their use of private revelation or contemporary prophecies, these go outside the revealed word of God and the audience has no ability to verify that it is even God speaking, let alone a foretelling of future events. Charismatic prophecies have come and gone without coming to pass and make a poor platform upon which to stand. The reductionist view that Charismatics hold on the written word of God should show the lack of validity in anything they proclaim. Revelation as we know it has ceased and therefore to use anything they might prophesy would be going outside the bounds of scripture and into error headlong.

The problem and danger of each of these focuses is that there is no way to validate and authenticate their veracity. The end-timer wants to show that the evil leaders of the current culture are the antichrist, while the charismatic is foretelling events not even in scripture. One goes outside interpretive rules while the other does not even bother with proper biblical exegesis, which tells us that revelation and private prophecies or words of knowledge have ceased. The end-timer cannot validate his interpretation of future events or the charismatic his own dreams of end-time events.

In the chapter on discernment, we will study this more specifically. One needs to be warned, however, that to listen to teachers who admonish us to "follow the spirit" and do not obey the Spirit of God, who tells us to "Study to show thyself approved to God, a workman that need not to be ashamed, rightly dividing the word of truth" (2 Tim 2:15), is to go against God's plain and clear word. We are to verify all these teachings against the light of scripture, exposing the false and holding fast to that which is good.

Two Classes of Christians

35. *As we are taught, the new prophets and apostles' "anointing" relegates them into a special group that does not command them to be accurate with their words from the Lord, nor accountable to his Church, nor validated by his written word.*

36. *These men walk around in their white suits flashing the anointing over sections of the stadium. Pretenders! That's all they are. They are charlatans spreading a false gospel that is not the gospel of the Bible.*

37. *They pretend to talk of sin but continue in their evil and wicked ways. And if we were to say anything against them, these white-suited hypocrites command us, "Do not touch the Lord's anointed."*

38. *The anointing is not to be thrown around like some fireball for entertainment and emotionalism as is seen in today's evangelistic meetings.*

39. *It is ironic that Jesus rebuked the Pharisees, calling them whitewashed sepulchers, when these deceiving preachers wear nice white suits and dresses.*

40. *We are told we need "a deeper anointing to understand the hidden things of God." The anointing is no different for the simplest new believer than for the most eloquent of preachers when they are both doing the work God has called them to. The file clerk sharing his or her faith is as anointed as the theologian giving his discourse to seminary students when they are fulfilling God's plan for their lives.*

41. *To tell us, "Do not touch the Lord's anointed" is to wrest and twist scripture from its true meaning.*

42. *We run to men, mere humans, for their touch. Thousands flock to revival meetings and hope to be touched by the "anointed preacher" and get their healing from him instead of to our God who is all sufficient and all powerful, by and through whom we have our very being.*

43. *The Roman church tells us we have to go to Mary or one of the saints while preachers today tell us to come to some stadium where they will be to experience the move of God because they are the "anointed of God."*

"Come and hear the most anointed prophet and preacher in the world today," reads the brochure for the latest seminar. This preacher or that evangelist is touted as the latest "anointed one" who stands beyond his peers because of a special endowment from God. Has God placed "favored son" status on certain individuals? In the New Testament, who is the "anointed one"? Are there true Christians who are not "anointed"? The biblical answers to these questions may surprise you.

In the Old Testament, "anointing" was often given to those specially set apart for a special office or task, such as that of a prophet, priest, or king. The idea of not "touching" an anointed individual can be seen with David in regard to Saul (e.g., 1 Sam 24 and 26). However, the context makes it very clear that what David meant was that Saul was not to be harmed *physically* because he was still God's anointed king (1 Sam 24:5–7; 26:9, 11, 23–24). It did *not* mean that Saul could not be criticized for failing to be faithful to God and his word—for in these very chapters David publicly rebukes the king on numerous occasions (see 1 Sam 24:8–21; 26:17–22).

Further proof that David did not take this as argument against criticism can be seen in Nathan's rebuke of his adultery and murder. David did not tell Nathan, "Do not touch the Lord's anointed," but rather accepted his rebuke in humble repentance (2 Sam 12:1–15)! Hence it is clear that this phrase does not have anything to do with scriptural criticism!

This understanding is also confirmed in Psalm 105:15, which is another much misused text. It reads, "Touch not my anointed ones, do my prophets no harm!" However, when one reads the context in which the passage occurs, it becomes clear that this refers to God's protection of his "anointed" Israel (and her prophets) from hostile nations during the time of the Exodus and settlement in Canaan. Even here God and his prophets are not slow to criticize "anointed" Israel for her waywardness! In conclusion, then, the Old Testament context shows that "not to touch the Lord's anointed" consistently refers to protection from *physical harm and never implies freedom from criticism or accountability.*

This outpouring of the Spirit to all is one of the great blessings of the New Covenant. Therefore, for some leaders to claim for themselves a unique "anointing" over and above that of others is presumptuous and puts them in danger of usurping Christ's place as the anointed one in the life of the believer. This teaching also separates the "haves" from the "have nots" and by consequence creates a two-tiered Christian community—the anointed ones and the ones who want the anointing. Disregarding the fact that all believers have the anointing, they either brush off scriptural teaching or just do not bother to inform their congregations of the fact.

In addition to this, scripture states that this anointing all believers have comes through the truth of the word by the Spirit (1 John 2:20–21, 27). Hence, one can validly argue that those who oppose themselves to the truth are in danger of "harming the Lord's anointed" people—even spurning Christ (the anointed one) himself (Acts 9:4; cf. Matt 25:40–45)!

What do today's modern prophets and anointed teachers say about this?

A Word of Faith preacher once stated:

> You cannot win attacking the servants of the Lord, no matter who they are or what they've done ... if the anointing ever comes upon a man, do not touch that man, even if he turns away from God, and serves the devil. Do not touch him. You are in deep, serious danger.[1]

However, we do not go by what man says but what God says. Where then do we find God speaking to us today? The only sure source of God's voice is the written word. It is the only source of objective truth that we have and our only source of verifying what we hear from the pulpit. So, what does the Bible mean when it says not to touch God's anointed and do his prophets no harm?

---

1. Hinn (Trinity Broadcast, 1999).

Two Classes of Christians

There are several verses in the Old Testament that speak about the "Lord's anointed."

1. In 1 Samuel 12:3–5; 24:6, 10; 26:9, 11, 16, 23; and 2 Samuel 1:14, 16; 19:21 it is a reference to the *kings* of Israel.
2. In Psalm 20:6, the "anointed" *king* is the divinely appointed means of the Lord's deliverance.
3. In Lamentations 4:20, it either refers to the nation of Israel as a whole or the king at the time of the Babylonian invasion.
4. Luke 7:37–38 speaks of the anointing as an act of love.
5. It was used for consecration of high priest, kings, and prophets (Exod 29:7; 1 Sam 9:16; 1 Kgs 19:16).
6. It is primarily figurative of Christ's kingly and priestly office (Ps 45:7; Ps 89:20; Isa 61:1; Acts 10:38; Heb 1:9), of spiritual gifts (2 Cor 1:21; 1 John 2:20, 27), and symbolic of Jesus (Matt 26:7–12; John 12:3–7).

The anointing was not the "power of God" but an act of consecration or being set aside. In the Old Testament, the anointing separated men out for specific offices—that of prophet, priest, and king. In the New Testament, all believers are said to be anointed. It is no longer set apart for the special few; now all who are of the elect also have the anointing.

> And it is God who establishes us with you in Christ, and has anointed us. (2 Cor 1:21)

> But you have an anointing from the Holy One, and you know all things. (1 John 2:20)

> And as for you, the anointing which you have received from him abides in you, and you have no need that anyone teach you; but as the same anointing teaches you concerning all things, and is true, and is not a lie, and just as it has taught you, you will abide in him. (1 John 2:27)

From these verses there could be no clearer message . . . The whole body of Christ is "anointed." It is not left for special Christians or super Christians; all have the same anointing, the same Holy Spirit. Unfortunately, charismatics, Pentecostals, and Word of Faith adherents have made the anointing a separate power that God gives to certain people. They have also made the "anointing" a thing, when scripture clearly tells us that the "anointing teaches" us and must therefore be a person, which indeed is the third person of the Trinity, the Holy Spirit.

But so confused are these teachers that a myriad of various anointings have been designed. The website *inplainsite.org* has an outstanding article on the "anointing" in which they have delineated several of them. Many they have reported on are "a swimming anointing," "the hurricane anointing," a TV anointing (which enables the anointed preacher to reach out to the television audience and if they place their hands on the screen, the anointing will be transferred to them for whatever ails them), the seed anointing, Rambo anointing, jubilee anointing, anointing of increase, fire anointing, anointed songs, trinkets, handkerchiefs, cornbread, candles, etc. However, when I tried to find these anointings in the scripture, they were not there.

When someone says they are "anointed" or "led by the Spirit" but consistently teach things contrary to the word in its accurate context, you can be assured that they're not being led by God's Spirit nor is the truth in them. Furthermore, if you are really anointed, you do not have to make threats, since it is God who protects his anointed. The word says, "Now I know that the LORD saves his anointed; he will answer him from his holy heaven with the saving might of his right hand. Some trust in chariots, and some in horses, but we trust in the name of the LORD our God" (Ps 20:6–7).

These supposed prophets have the audacity to state that doctrine is not necessary, that the formation of the local church structure is to be done away with. One such "prophet" said:

> We are in a season of great transition. Transitioning out of old doctrine, old structure, religious mindsets and religion . . .[2]

She continues by stating that for the last two thousand years, the Church has been a "religious movement" and now suddenly we will be saints. It should puzzle one familiar with scripture to be told that only now we are in a "saints movement"[3] when the word of God states in almost every epistle written that they were being sent to "saints." Christianity has always been about relationship—the Father sending his Son to die for his people. We are in relationship with the Father because of Jesus Christ the

---
2. Freed, *Get the Anointing Out of the Box*.
3. Freed, "Get the Anointing Out of the Box," (accessed July 12, 2007).

Two Classes of Christians

Son. God's people have always been his children and he our Father. There is no greater relationship than that between child and Father.

Further, these supposed apostles and super apostles state that they are needed in order to "take people (to places) because they are pioneering cutting edge anointing that understand the purposes, plans, and counsel of God" because only they "have insight into the revelation knowledge of God."[4]

So, these new apostles and prophets have taken on the Gnostic idea of "special knowledge," "special positions," and "special revelations" over and above the written, revealed word of God. They continue to claim a "new work" of God, relegating two thousand years of Church history to the circular file (garbage can) and place themselves above Peter, Paul, and even Jesus himself. This section will end with their own words, for by them they condemn themselves and show their teachings to be heretical and themselves false prophets.

> The *New Apostolic Reformation* is an extraordinary work of the Holy Spirit that is *changing the shape of Christianity globally*. It is truly a new day! The Church is changing. New names! New methods! New worship expressions! The Lord is *establishing the foundations* of the Church for the new millennium. This foundation is built upon *Apostles and Prophets*. Apostles execute and establish *God's plan* on the earth.[5]

> Apostles and prophets are the foundation of the Church and, um, I identify as James an apostle as my function as *a horizontal apostle to bring together the people of the body of Christ*. Not only can I do it, I love to do it. Yesterday I was the apostle with a group of about fifteen to twenty prophets. We met all day long, and these prophets, many of whom are going to be speakers in this conference, come under my guidance, coordination, and leadership as an apostle. They each have apostles in their own networks but I mean they are under spiritually. But *I'm the one that brings them together*, and when I bring them together things happen.[6]

> *No prophet or apostle who ever lived equalled the power* of these individuals in this great army of the Lord in these last days. No one

---

4. Eckhart, *Moving in the Apostolic*.
5. Wagner, "National Apostolic-Prophetic Conference," (accessed 17 July 2007).
6. Wagner, "National School of the Prophets—Mobilizing the Prophetic Office," (accessed July 16, 2007).

ever had it, not even Elijah or Peter or Paul, or anyone else enjoyed the power that is gong to rest on this great army.[7]

Paul rebukes them with the following words:

> And what I do I will continue to do, in order to undermine the claim of those who would like to claim that in their boasted mission they work on the same terms as we do. For such men are false apostles, deceitful workmen, disguising themselves as apostles of Christ. And no wonder, for even Satan disguises himself as an angel of light. So it is no surprise if his servants, also, disguise themselves as servants of righteousness. Their end will correspond to their deeds. (2 Cor 11:12–15)

There is a certain prophet and preacher whom most who have ever watched televangelism are certainly aware of. He parades around throwing the "anointing" as if it were a baseball or dodge ball. Usually the scenario goes like this: The crowd has been worked into an emotionalist state through the music and lights. The preacher has come out to the stage with the song "How Great Thou Art." A short devotional about the "new move of God" has been preached, possibly a prophecy about the city he is in and how God will send revival to them in one, two, or three years depending (funny how God doesn't know quite when that revival will come). The offering has been taken (always before the miracles occur), and those with supposed miracles have made their way to the stage. Aches and pains have been healed, for you never see restored limbs or perfectly restored hearing or eyesight. Instead things such as fibromyalgia are suddenly healed, and then the person is touched and down they go. Then, not too far into the meeting, suddenly the anointed preacher will decide to throw the "fire anointing" on the catchers (those who stand behind the person being healed just in case, and it's rare that they do not fall backwards) or the audience (just the first few rows, though) or the pastors lined up on the stage, and down they go.

I had occasion several years ago to attend a miracle crusade with a pastor I was employed with. He had the "honor" of being allowed on the stage and having the "fire" thrown on him. When asked what occurred and what he felt, he just ignored me and laughed, then turned away and mumbled, "I got knocked down." Why could there be no explanation?

---

7. Simpson, "False Prophets," (accessed July 17, 2007). Quote from Bob Jones and Paul Cain. "Selections from the Kansas City Prophets" audiotape (tape:155C).

Two Classes of Christians

Why no testimony about what he felt, if he felt anything? Because nothing happened... pure emotionalism.

His white suit picked out by floodlights, this United States-based preacher promised a "miracle crusade" to heal the sick, make the blind see, and make the lame walk. "In Jesus' name, lift your hands and sing!" he cried, almost drowned out by cheering.[8]

From one of the early leaders of the Vineyard movement, it is acknowledged that these types of "anointed" displays cannot be found in scripture. Let's read it from their own leader.

> There's no place in the Bible where people were lined up and Jesus or Paul or anyone else went along and bopped them on the head and watched them go down, one after another, and somebody else ran along behind. Can you picture Peter and James—"Hold it, hold it, hold it!"—running along behind trying to catch them? And so the model that we're seeing, either on stage or on television, is totally different from anything that's in scripture.[9]

While reviewing this section, I was emailed the following article with regard to the prosperous nature of the apostolic and prophetic movement.

> *GOD DOLLARS*
> America's preachers have long grasped the potential material rewards of their spiritual gifts. (*Name withheld*) has said he earns up to US$1 million a year, lives in a US$10 million seaside mansion and owns a private jet. (*Name withheld*), who visited Uganda this month, drives a Rolls Royce.
>
> Africa's preachers are learning fast. At Uganda's Holy Fire Ministry—a marquee beside a dirt track near the airport—hundreds line up for blessings from 'prophet' Pius Muwanguzi, whose purported talents include curing AIDS by touching the forehead.
>
> In the kneeling congregation: a polio victim, a blind man and a girl who lost her phone.
>
> The pastor touches an old woman, she faints. Then out come the collection envelopes. Minimum is 100,000 Uganda shillings (US$62.5) the poor can give as little as 10,000 to receive a blessing. Muwanguzi, whose own blessings include a smart suit and a new Toyota Land Cruiser, declined an interview. But his secretary Jackie Kamanyire said payments were voluntary.

---

8. Reuters, "Pentecostals Buckle up Africa's Bible Belt," *Jamaica Gleaner*.
9. Wimber, *Spiritual Phenomena: Slain in the Spirit*.

> "If you feel like sowing a seed, you sow. It comes from your heart. The prophet cures AIDS, cancer and sickle cell disease with his blessings."
>
> Cameroon's Pierre Anatole Mbezele, who stages miracles at his Yaounde church, gets showered with lavish gifts, including, on two occasions, a Mercedes- Benz.
>
> Francis Adroa gave her car to a Ugandan church promising to cure her of HIV/AIDS. The miracle failed, she got sicker. And now she's a pedestrian.
>
> Moses Malay heads a Ugandan organisation helping what he calls victims of 'pulpit fraud' after quitting a church whose pastor claimed divine powers.
>
> "I saw people robbed and I participated. How do they do it? Simple. They instil hope, they nurture it, they reap."[10]

There are several points to remember with regard to specifically the throwing of "the anointing" and several other Charismatic-specific teachings:

- An "anointed" preacher *"throwing the anointing over the crowds"* is an *exact* parallel to the actions of the power gurus—with the same resulting manifestations.

- The manifestations at Toronto and Pensacola are an *exact* parallel to those in people having the serpent power awakened in them.

- In both camps people obtain these manifestations through the laying on of hands, via impartation of an anointed individual.[11]

> For the last several years, the Church has begun to practice a new paradigm (which is a new way of practicing Christianity). Although it was birthed in Pentecostalism, it has crossed denominational boundaries. It has literally changed biblical traditions for what is now called a new thing of the Spirit. ("God is doing a new thing.")[12]

If anyone has watched a particular televangelist's crusades, it is sure you have not missed this person throwing the "anointing" into the crowd, directly onto individuals and small groupings of people. Many describe

---

10. Ibid.
11. "Hindu Gurus and Pentecostal Preachers are Identical," (accessed July 6, 2007).
12. "The New Violence of the Holy Spirit?," (accessed July 4, 2007).

being hit with a force that is strong enough to knock them over. One of the leading promoters of this activity describes this as:

> Instantly, the power of God hit the place. People began to cry and many fell to the floor ... as I turned and pointed toward him, he fell backward several feet. I was trying to get him to come close and suddenly he was farther away.[13]

Another preacher describes it in this way: "It is tangible. It can be felt. Just as electricity is tangible, so is the anointing." Not only is it solid and touchable but transferable. You can communicate it, and you can give it away. You can store it up, and you can give it away. "The anointing of God as wonderful as it is electricity."

Yet another describes what she interpreted as a visitation from God "... I got up and started stepping over bodies and putting my hand next to them. I could feel the power, like heat or electricity, radiating off their bodies."[14]

> To John it was spiritual power came from his hands like electricity.[15]

Since when is the third person of the Trinity referred to as "electricity" or "heat"? When did the person of the Holy Spirit become a non-person, an "it"? Are we to follow the erroneous footsteps of the Jehovah's Witnesses when referring to God the Spirit? Should we abandon the Bible's teaching on the personhood of the Spirit and make him an it? To do so is to remove oneself from orthodox Christianity, from historical Christian teaching, and from the true Church of Jesus Christ.

To further display their heretical and repulsive teachings, I will include a part of an article from a prominent Charismatic magazine whose own editor is getting frustrated with the extremes that are being accepted without even the slightest discernment among those who claim to be the people of God.

> At a Charismatic conference in an East Coast city recently, a pastor stood on a stage in front of a large crowd and smugly announced that the guest speaker was "more than an apostle." Then the host asked everyone to bow down to the person, claiming that this posture was necessary to release God's power.

---

13. Hinn, *The Anointing*, 27.
14. Hanegraaff, *Counterfeit Revival* 200.
15. Ibid, 204

"This is the only way you can receive this kind of anointing!" the host declared, bowing in front of the speaker. Immediately, about 80 percent of the audience fell prostrate on the floor.[16]

Yet, time and again, people attend their meetings, conferences, crusades, and worship services, and they speak of the Holy Spirit as "the anointing" or "fire" or whatever moves them in particular at that moment. The work of the Holy Spirit is to convince and convict people of sin and regenerate them so that they may respond to the call of the gospel. His role is not to make us quiver or shake, fall down, roll over, slither, bark like a dog, or get into a birthing position on the floor so that we may birth new ministries. God the Spirit's role in the plan of redemption is to bring in those whom the Father has chosen and for whom Christ died.

At these meetings it is very *rare* that you will hear the *biblical message of salvation: repent and believe.* Instead, you will be told to "choose Jesus" or "come and receive Jesus." There is no call to turn from your sin and turn to Jesus in repentance to trust that his good works are the only good works that will count for your salvation or that his life and death satisfied the law of God for you so that his righteousness is imputed to your account and you are made just before the Lord. This is the gospel that must be given at every gathering of Christians. Luther said that we are apt to forget this crucial truth and therefore we need a daily reminder so that we never trust our good works to merit anything from the Lord. It would do the Christian Church well to again remember daily the true gospel and rest in the righteousness of Christ for our justification.

---

16. Grady, "The Deadly Virus of Celebrity Christianity," July 2007.

5

Down They Go . . . Again!

44. *The only ones who fell down in scripture were those in the presence of God (who fell forward) and those who came to arrest our Lord (who fell backward).*

45. *Only those who fell forward were true servants of the most high. The only exception is John the beloved. None other in the New Testament era is said to have fallen down before Christ.*

46. *Nowhere in scripture do we find Peter, Paul, or any of the apostles, nor Isaiah, Jeremiah, Ezekiel, or any of the Old Testament prophets telling of electricity going through their bodies or being "drained" from the anointing.*

> The New Testament, which is our perfect pattern, records no events where a minister caused people to fall on the floor. This particular phenomenon appears, from my research, to have actually commenced with Miss Kuhlman and a handful of other healing evangelists . . . Usually the person was caught by those who were called catchers . . . and they remained on the floor only briefly. *With (name withheld), there appeared no distinction as to who was slain, including Jewish Rabbis, Catholic priests and nuns, unsaved individuals, or simply whosoever might get . . . special prayer.*[1]

That in itself is enough to forever settle the absence of validity and biblical support. The Holy Spirit never acts indiscriminately in his holy touch on human lives. Second, whatever he does brings honor only to Jesus Christ and always has deep and profound purpose. The Kingdom of God does not play with human emotions and sensational activities. The overwhelm-

1. Chambers, *Kathryn Kuhlman & Her Spirit Guide*, 8.

ing factor is that this questionable phenomenon has spread all over the Church world and has followed exactly the pattern commenced by her (*name withheld*).

> (*Name withheld*) actually tells of an individual slain in the Spirit with a cigarette in his mouth.[2]

If we are to believe the accounts of slaying in the Spirit, we must, as we have seen with each previous example, test it in the light of scripture. So let us look at instances of people falling down in the word of God and see if we can learn anything about this in a proper manner. Let's begin with some examples from the New Testament.

NEW TESTAMENT EXAMPLES OF PEOPLE FALLING DOWN

1. Believers on occasion would fall down before Jesus in worship.

Matthew 2:11:

> And going into the house they saw the child with Mary his mother, and they fell down and worshiped him. Then, opening their treasures, they offered him gifts, gold and frankincense and myrrh.

First Corinthians 14:24–25:

> But if all prophesy, and an unbeliever or outsider enters, he is convicted by all, he is called to account by all, the secrets of his heart are disclosed, and so, falling on his face, he will worship God and declare that God is really among you.

While there are several instances of people coming to Jesus and falling at his feet, it is usually in a voluntary mode of worship. Scenarios typically used by adherents of this extra-biblical doctrine are when Mary came to Jesus at the death of Lazarus and "fell down at his feet" (John 11:32), as well as the leper who was healed in Luke 17:16. The term "fall down" or "fell down" is used in scripture to primarily describe their act of worship and obedience. These who fell down before the Lord were all coming to him as believers looking for his healing touch or worshipping him for who he is. There is *no* account in the scriptures of any *believer* falling backward either before Jesus or any of the apostles or prophets.

---

2. Ibid.

Down They Go ... Again!

2. Another instance of falling down is found in the account of the transfiguration of Christ.

I would like you to note clearly that Jesus did not touch them and they fell, but instead, when he touched them, they rose to their feet. This is exactly *opposite* of what occurs in the Pentecostal/Charismatic services, conference or crusades.

Matthew 17:1–7:

> And after six days Jesus took with him Peter and James, and John his brother, and led them up a high mountain by themselves. And he was transfigured before them, and his face shone like the sun, and his clothes became white as light. And behold, there appeared to them Moses and Elijah, talking with him. And Peter said to Jesus, "Lord, it is good that we are here. If you wish, I will make three tents here, one for you and one for Moses and one for Elijah." he was still speaking when, behold, a bright cloud overshadowed them, and a voice from the cloud said, "This is my beloved Son, with whom I am well pleased; listen to him." When the disciples heard this, they fell on their faces and were terrified. But Jesus came and touched them, saying, "Rise, and have no fear."

What is the reason they fell? They were terrified and were trying to hide. There was no "slaying of the Spirit" here. These men had just seen Jesus in all his glory and they panicked and took the only position natural to man in fear, the fetal position on the ground. When Jesus saw them, he then touched them, and they rose to their feet. This is not what occurs at these meetings, but indeed, the opposite occurs with the person falling when the "anointed" preacher touches him or her. Do not be fooled. Those on the stages of today's miracles crusades who fall have not seen the transfigured Christ but have been goaded into falling.

Jamie Buckingham, one of (*name withheld*)'s biographers admitted that toward the end of her life the "anointing" was often nonexistent. He tells the story here:

> She (*name withheld*) was moving back and forth across the state, saying all her favorite phrases. They seemed empty. The singer had climbed to her feet and (she) touched her again. Nothing happened this time. In a desperate move I heard her say, "The Spirit is all over you, Jamie." She swept toward me, putting her hands on my jaw as I sang. There had been times in the past when, if she even

> got close to me, I would go down "under the power." But that day it was just (her)—with her hands on my jaw. I loved her too much to disappoint her. With a sigh of resignation, I fell backward into the arms of the man behind me.[3]

Should it surprise us then that these so-called anointed people actually begin to pretend to have the move of God on them? Should this concern us? Or do we merely walk away from this and only see what we want to see? The Church today is being deceived and willingly falling for it hook, line, and sinker.

Those who were enemies of God, unbelievers, and outright antagonists are all recorded as having fallen backward. When pointing this out to several people who are in the Charismatic circle, they begin to make excuses such as, "Well, people are afraid to fall on their faces." "Preachers do not want to get sued over someone hurting themselves by falling on their faces . . ." and other outrageous comments. First, these preachers tell us that the people falling are under the utter control of the Holy Spirit. So the Holy Spirit doesn't want to get sued? He doesn't want to hurt people? He's trying to be "legally correct" about the whole thing? That is utterly ridiculous. We've already seen that primarily the people who fell on their faces in the Bible were not "under the power" but from their own will and volition fell before the Lord face forward. Do we conclude, then, that those falling backward are also doing so of their own will and volition? Quite possibly so.

Let's look at some examples of the enemies of Christ.

3. The men who took Jesus in the Garden of Gethsemane fell back when he said the words, "I am he."

John 18:1–7:

> When Jesus had spoken these words, he went out with his disciples across the Kidron Valley, where there was a garden, which he and his disciples entered. Now Judas, who betrayed him, also knew the place, for Jesus often met there with his disciples. So Judas, having procured a band of soldiers and some officers from the chief priests and the Pharisees, went there with lanterns and torches and weapons. Then Jesus, knowing all that would happen to him, came forward and said to them, "Whom do you seek?" They answered him, "Jesus of Nazareth." Jesus said to them, "I am he." Judas, who

---

3. Buckingham, *Daughter of Destiny: Kathryn Kuhlman, Her Story*, 281.

betrayed him, was standing with them. When Jesus said to them, "I am he," *they drew back and fell to the ground.* So he asked them again, "Whom do you seek?" And they said, "Jesus of Nazareth."

Matthew Henry comments on verse 6 in this way:

> *They went backward, and,* like men thunder-struck, *fell to the ground.* It should seem, they did not fall forward, as humbling themselves before him, and yielding to him, but backward, as standing it out to the utmost. Thus Christ was declared to be more than a man, even when he was trampled upon as *a worm, and no man.* This word, *I am he,* had revived his disciples, and raised them up (Matt 14:27); but the same word strikes his enemies down.[4]

The Lord chose to give them this proof of his infinite power so they might know that their power could not prevail against him if he chose to exert his might, seeing that the very breath of his mouth confused, drove back, and struck them down to the earth.

4. Saul fell down to the ground when the Risen Savior appeared to him on the road to Damascus.

Next we come to the account of the apostle Paul at his conversion, while he was still known as Saul.

Acts 9:4–6:

> And *falling to the ground he heard a voice* saying to him, "Saul, Saul, why are you persecuting me?" And he said, "Who are you, Lord?" And he said, "I am Jesus, whom you are persecuting. But rise and enter the city, and you will be told what you are to do." (emphasis added)

While we cannot be sure as to whether Saul fell backward or forward, we are assured of this: he fell down on the ground in utter fear. Not only did Saul see a light from heaven, but he also heard a voice from there. *Whenever God shows his glory, the word of God is heard as well. God's manifestations of himself are never dumb shows, done for the fleshly and carnal desires of men and women, for he magnifies his word above all his name, and what was seen was always designed to make way for what was said.*

---

4. Henry, *A Commentary on the Holy Bible.*

5. Ananias fell down dead when he was struck by God for lying to the Holy Spirit.

We come now to one who was a clear enemy of God, for he and his wife conspired to lie to the Holy Spirit. One should notice clearly that he fell down, but he also died.

Acts 5:3–5:

> But Peter said, "Ananias, why has Satan filled your heart to lie to the Holy Spirit and to keep back for yourself part of the proceeds of the land? While it remained unsold, did it not remain your own? And after it was sold, was it not at your disposal? Why is it that you have contrived this deed in your heart? You have not lied to men but to God." When Ananias heard these words, he fell down and breathed his last. And great fear came upon all who heard of it.

Not much explanation is needed on this account except that it should be noted that the Holy Spirit was not going to allow the dignity of the Godhead to be denigrated, and therefore judgment came to Ananias and his wife Sapphira later that day.

A singular event:

6. John fell at Christ's feet "as dead" in Rev. 1:17.

It is imperative for any student of the Bible to understand proper exegesis (explanation) of scriptural texts. You never take a singular event or verse and create a doctrine about it. Here we have the account of John the apostle falling down "as dead" before the resurrected and glorified Savior, Jesus Christ. John is seeing Jesus no longer in a transfigured form but in the fullness of his glory.

> The terrible splendour of such majesty was more than the apostle could bear, and he fell down deprived of his senses, but was soon enabled to behold the vision by a communication of strength from our Lord's right hand.[5]

Yet, time and time again, modern-day prophets and "anointed preachers" will use this as an example of what happens when they pray

---

5. Clarke, *The Holy Bible, Containing the Old and New Testaments, the Text Carefully Printed from the Most Correct Copies of the Present Authorized Translation, Including the Marginal Readings and Parallel Texts: With a Commentary and Critical Notes Designed as a Help to a Better Understanding of the Sacred Writings.*

for people. However, when those people fall down, is it because they have seen Jesus in the fullness of his glory? Is it because they are about to be given some final revelation? Well, unfortunately, since these teachers believe and instruct their followers that there is continued revelation, they probably claim they do.

HOW ARE THESE EXAMPLES DIFFERENT FROM CHARISMATIC "SPIRIT SLAYING"?[6]

The instances of falling down in the New Testament have *no similarity whatsoever with the "Spirit slaying" phenomenon that is a part with the Charismatic movement*. First of all, in the New Testament there was no laying on of hands preceding the falling down. In fact, there was no human participation in any of the instances of falling in the Bible. In the instance shown at the mount of transfiguration, Jesus touches them after they've fallen and then they stand up.

Second, there was no convulsive jerking. There are no reports of an electric charge going through anyone. We do not read of anyone shaking, quaking, or rolling on the floor in an epileptic manner. If they fell, they fell "as dead" and did not get up until Christ brought them up. There is no record in the scriptures of this type of phenomena.

Third, there was no laughter connected with the falling; instead we find fear or awe. We read of people fearing God, trembling, and scared, but not of anyone laughing. There is no record in the written word of God that anyone laughed in the presence of God. In fact, the warning is that those who laugh now will weep later (cf. Luke 6:21, 25). Sarah laughed at the news that she would bear a son for Abraham but tried to cover up her incredulity. This laughing was not from the Lord or else why cover it up if the Lord had given it to her?

Fourth, no one who fell was pulled up and then fell again only to have Jesus pick them up again so he could "slay" them. People who fell down and worshipped the Lord, when once brought to their feet, did not once again fall. This idea of picking up someone slain in the Spirit and then knocking them down again is nothing more than showmanship and degrading the Spirit of God. There is no record in scripture of people falling over in a drunken stupor created by God. The call is to be sober and vigilant, not drunk in the Spirit.

6. Cloud, "Confusion about 'Spirit Slaying,'" May 10, 2006.

Fifth, there was no mood or tone set to encourage falling. There was no teaching about falling. There were no people lining up waiting to fall. There were no repetitive choruses preparing people for mystical or Gnostic experiences. There were no light shows, emotional songs, and hype to get people to fall before the Lord. In fact, there was primarily fear and sometimes repentance as in the case of Isaiah and Saul/Paul. There was no one yelling "Fire!" or "Fire on ya!" or any such thing.

> If you have had some sort of sensual experience like falling on your back due to some kind of "impartation"—a term the Bible does not use nor promote nor teach by example as a normal Christian experience; or exhibited some kind of "manifestation"—a term used only once in the Bible with regards to the gifts of the Spirit which are clearly listed (1 Cor. 12:7–11); been in an induced trance state, found yourself pinned to the floor, laughed uncontrollably, made animal noises, exhibited signs of "drunkenness in the spirit," or other such phenomena . . . if you have "experienced" these things . . . has the urge to pass along those experiences taken on more importance than preaching the gospel? Have they begun to overshadow the word of God and its sound doctrines and their application to your life? Have they taken on more significance than the sanctifying ethical work of the Holy Spirit in your life? Have they begun to eclipse the work of the cross in your relationship with Jesus Christ of Nazareth, to whom the Holy Spirit always points our worship and obedience? Are you now a zealous proponent of something you have not really investigated fully but only "experienced"? Examine yourself and others in your congregation to see if phenomena such as "slain in the spirit" have taken on far more importance in your life than they should.[7]

The above quote is of great importance in our day of pragmatism. We live in a post-modern world where truth is relative to the individual's experience, culture, and demographics. However, scripture is not subjective truth. In fact, it is the only source of objective truth that God has given to us. We can verify teachings, doctrine, and experience by the light of the word of God because it is *inerrant, infallible, inspired,* and *uncorrupted.* Our experiences *change* from day to day and from mood to mood.

Any experience that cannot be found in scripture can then not be verified by scripture because it is outside of the written, revealed word. Since it cannot be verified to be actual acts of God, how then do we verify it as

---

7. Prasch, *Slain in the Spirit: A Midrashic Perspective.*

Down They Go . . . Again!

being a "move of the Spirit"? We'd have nothing to gauge it by and that leaves us open to other moves, which may be anathema to one generation of Christians and widely accepted by a later generation. Reader, if it is not in scripture, there is no way to make absolute sure it is of God. Therefore, if we cannot verify it, then we must not teach it, practice it, or believe it; in fact, we must denounce it.

If we allow one thing to come into the Church that is not prescribed by God in his word, how do we stop other unverifiable "experiences"? We would be left to each man judging for himself whether something is right . . . and we know what Judges says about the results of every man deciding for himself what is right. We'd be in a bigger bog than we are now in American evangelicalism.

Take courage, though, because the word of God is established, unchangeable, and unmovable. We cannot, we dare not, base our interpretations of experiences upon what the majority is doing as the majority is often, if not always, wrong. We must base our beliefs and view our experiences through the critical lens of scripture alone.

6

Just a Little Discernment, Please!

47. *Christians are to be taught that many who claim to be sheep are nothing more than wolves in sheep's clothing.*

48. *Warned not to judge, they forget that we are to judge angels and are therefore commanded to judge those who profess to be believers.*

49. *Instead of obeying Paul's command to preach the word in season and out, these self-declared prophets twist the words of Christ to gain power, prestige, and prominence, all the while crying that their ministries are suffering.*

Throw away your charts and theology and let's get stupid for Jesus.[1]

Hardly can one watch what is called "Christian television" without hearing the ideas of studying scripture downgraded and belittled. Most of these preachers will tell you that you just need "an anointing" from the "spirit" and you can forget the diligent study of the scriptures. You can ignore the implicit commands to "study" and to "meditate" on the word of God because either the "spirit will reveal everything to you" or they will inform you of deep truths and revelations. However, you should not get bogged down in theology, otherwise you will end up with a "religious spirit" that will need to be cast out of you. So goes today's teachings from television to the pulpits. Anyone who dares to research what is taught is accused of not being open to the Spirit and having a demonic spirit themselves. Anyone who challenges these so-called preachers and teachers is immediately reduced to an "unbeliever" or "heretic hunter." They are relegated to those who "do not understand" or are caught up in too much learning. They are to be pitied, according to the televangelists.

1. Lehman, Blue Mountain Christian Retreat, Tape 1, Session 1.

Just a Little Discernment, Please!

Once again, the question must be asked, "What do the scriptures say?"

> But in your hearts honor Christ the Lord as holy, always being prepared to make a defense to anyone who asks you for a reason for the hope that is in you. (1 Pet 3:15)

> Do your best to present yourself to God as one approved, a worker who has no need to be ashamed, rightly handling the word of truth. (2 Tim 2:15)

Though scripture verifies that saving faith is a gift from God, nevertheless, faith comes by hearing and hearing by the word of God. It is in the word of God that we are given proofs of the validity of the faith. Paul argues with the Corinthians that eyewitnesses saw the Risen Christ and many were still alive at the time he was writing to them. Thomas was called to touch and see that Jesus was alive by putting his finger in the nail prints and his hand in Christ's side. These are calls to look at evidentiary facts as aids to believing. God has not made us stupid creatures but rational beings who think and process evidence. Rational evidence will not, most likely, be the catalyst for saving faith, nevertheless, is crucial to removing all objections and putting forth the true evidence for the Christian faith.

Pastors today are in danger of removing the credibility of Christianity by minimizing the necessity of defending the faith or proclaiming it in its objective totality. How do they handle the exhortation of the Apostle Peter to have a defense ready, an *apologia* in Greek, to answer for their faith? Through making Christianity a subjective faith, the pastors actually remove the objectiveness of the faith, thereby creating a faith based primarily, and sometimes even solely, on experience. Once that occurs, Christians lose the ability to offer definitive truth simply because the argument will come, "Well, that's your opinion." A solid defense of the scripture, based upon evidence, must be maintained so that an "apologia" may be given for why Christianity is believed and is logically the best answer to the questions of eternity.

TOOLS OF THE TRADE: THE NECESSITY OF DEFENDING

A Modern Ninety-Five

THE FAITH

Within the toolbox of Christianity there remains a tool very seldom taken out, let alone used. This tool lies at the bottom of the box and gathers dust at first and eventually, due to lack of use and care by the owners, becomes rusty and useless. Many Christians view this tool as being too specialized or difficult to master. They say, "Let those trained at the best schools and apprenticed in its function use it. We lay Christians will stick with the tools we know how to use." Or, they will tell us, "Do not use that tool. It's too sharp and you'll hurt your fellow Christian." This reminds me of the movie *A Christmas Story* where the child wanted a BB gun and his mother said, "You'll shoot your eye out." The tool I am speaking of is none other than that of apologetics or the science of defending the faith.

From observations I have made as I've spoken at many conferences, preached at crusades, and evangelized locally and in various parts of the world such as Guatemala, Mexico, Puerto Rico, Canada, and Ghana, I've seen that the majority of Christians do not even know this tool lays at the bottom of their toolbox, almost crying out, if it were animated, to be used more often, and yes, even daily. This tool is seen as too specialized and people believe that only those who have become masters of it, or earned Master's degrees in it, are authorized to wield its power. Many Christians believe that if people become too skilled with this tool, they may forget about the others they have become more comfortable with. Hence, the tool of apologetics remains at the bottom of most Christians' toolboxes and some have even discarded it, thinking it an antiquated tool or perhaps a tool that only the most highly skilled master craftsmen can handle.

When studying the various aspects of apologetics, one learns that there are traditionally two forms of it. The first, though not necessarily in order of prestige, power, or importance, is *irenics*. The second is *polemics*. However, often one may need to use a hybrid blend of the two styles of apologetics in the ministry of defending the faith against cultic influence coming from within the Church itself. It is a fight to defend from within against the disease of erroneous and heretical teachings and from without against the cultic teachings and pragmatic worldview systems.

Irenic apologetics is the practice of debating and discussing Christian doctrines with other Christians who are theologically orthodox but with whom there are matters of theological disagreement or dispute. It is the discussion of both key issues as well as practical issues within the Body of

Christ. This is usually a friendly debate between two differing viewpoints such as a discussion between a-millennialism, pre-millennialism, and post-millennialism. These are usually areas where both parties can vigorously debate their viewpoint and doctrine, arguing even loudly at times, yet at the end each party walks out hand in hand with a brother or sister in Christ knowing that these are not necessarily essential issues but reflect contrasting opinions within the community of faith.

Polemic apologetics is the aggressive disputation and refutation of another position or doctrine. It usually functions outside the Body of Christ and deals with attempting to show the superiority of Christian teaching over that of other religious beliefs. The means by which polemics is done is through a systematic and ordered setting down of the Christian system of belief, the uniformity of its doctrine and teachings, and it's congruence with human knowledge. This type of apologetics is usually engaged with someone from a cult or pseudo-Christian religion such as Jehovah's Witnesses, Church of the Latter Day Saints (Mormons), and Seventh-Day Adventists. It is also widely used for those with differing religions or worldviews such as naturalists, atheists, Marxists and Communists, and Muslims, to name a few.

Within the ministry, one must come to understand that both of these disciplines are necessary in defending true biblical Christianity. Very often when invited to a church where works are made the preeminent teaching or doctrine of salvation, a true understanding of the doctrine of justification by faith alone through Christ alone needs to be explained in a manner that is in the language of the audience to whom one is speaking. When speaking at a Pentecostal church, the discussion comes down to whether a saved woman can wear makeup or slacks. The discipline of irenics comes into play here because we are discussing an issue of belief, not doctrine, which might have, unfortunately, been elevated to a fruit of the Spirit that seeks prove whether or not a woman is saved by whether she wears skirts or slacks.

One approach is to question, "What does scripture teach on this subject?" However, due to the lack of true biblical teaching, many have not been taught the scriptures and take what was taught to them from the pulpit as inspired and infallible. They believe everything they are fed and walk out not knowing whether they have been given the manna from heaven or the poison of asps. Most, unfortunately, do not know the difference and of these the majority do not really care anymore as long as they feel good when they leave the worship service.

A place where apologetics enables one to be more efficient is the area of irenic/polemic debate within the Church. In today's pragmatic evangelical churches amongst pseudo-evangelicals speckled with strong influences of mysticism and Charismatica, the Church is being infiltrated by erroneous and heretical teachings by the droves. Today what passes from our pulpits is less truth and more error than probably at any other time in the history of Christianity.

In generations past, error came almost in singular waves. However, we are seeing in our generation wave upon wave coming against the true faith and not being stopped but actually welcomed with open arms into the Body of Christ. Where once debates regarding the deity and humanity of Christ were settled, once again Sabealliansim has reared its deceptive head among the Pentecostals we know as Oneness. The Mystics and Gnostics of the past have become regular fodder for the people of God through their massive television ministries and online teachings. Montanists run rampant again with their ongoing prophecies and continued revelations. Centuries ago these groups were considered heretics. Today, they are considered the "anointed" preachers and teachers.

Most Christians today do not understand defending the faith. They may understand it when the Jehovah's Witness rings their doorbell or when the Mormon boy missionaries in pristine white shirts, ties, and firmly pressed slacks offer them literature that says, "We're true believers." However, they do not comprehend when that error tracks its way into the Church more subtly, nor do they know how to recognize it when it does.

Os Guinness gave us the example of the frog in the pot. How do you cook a frog? If you place that frog in boiling water, it will jump out. So you set a pot of room temperature water on the stove, place the frog into the water, and then turn up the flame. The frog will swim around enjoying itself. However, as the water warms up, it is done so slowly that the frog never notices it is being cooked. That is the unfortunate state of the Church today. The errors have come in slowly and congregations have been milling around doing "their thing," completely oblivious to the fact that they've been "cooked."

Just a Little Discernment, Please!

When a supposed evangelist can say on television, "I am a 'little messiah' walking the earth,"[2] or "Are you ready for some real revelation knowledge . . . you are God,"[3] and thousands still flock to his crusades, then you know that Christians are not skilled in apologetics, let alone discernment. Teachings such as this and other heretical doctrines from the Word of Faith movement are gaining a foothold, no a stronghold, within even traditionally biblical denominations. Yet, there are relatively few who can actually and successfully refute these teachings and fewer still who care anymore.

Applying discernment to the defense of the faith both outside of orthodox Christianity with Mormons who teach the pre-existence of the soul and inside those same bounds with those of the Word of Faith Movement who claim to be orthodox yet teach the pre-existence of the soul, one can make a strong case for rejecting erroneous and dangerous teachings. (See example noted below.)

> I saw new lives of little babies singing and flying around God's Throne. It seemed to me that babies just came out of the breath of God. They looked like they were wearing nightgowns. They flew into the presence of Jehovah. I realized they were new souls who came from the thoughts of God. God thinks kids. Now I know why those newborn babies are so precious. Babies are gifts given to us directly from the Throne of God. I heard them saying to God, "Can I be a spirit? Would you send me to the earth so I can be a spirit? I want to be a redeemed person. Can I be a spirit?" And while I watched, I heard that mighty sound of God's power, Whooosh! I saw these babies leave the Throne by the power of God.[4]

Discernment and apologetics are not for the specialist; they are tools for every believer. Scripture tells us that all Christians should be able to "give an answer" for their faith. Christians are to be able to defend it from the onslaughts of cultists as well as the erroneous and heretical teachings coming through the majority television screens and radio programs that profess to be "evangelical." When we do not defend the faith, we allow error to run rampant and reap the result of our own laziness and idleness.

Recognize that you have an incredible tool the majority of believers do not even know exists or are too frightened to use. This apologetic tool

---

2. Hinn, *Praise-a-Thon on TBN* (11/6/1990).
3. Hinn, "Tape # A031190-1," in *Our Position in Christ*.
4. Duplantis, *Heaven: Close Encounters of the God Kind*, 119.

exists in your toolbox and must be taken out, dusted off, polished up, and sharpened by reading and studying scripture, commentaries, and the writings of educated men down through the centuries all the while relying upon the Holy Spirit to guide you into truth.

For the most part over the past ten years, our ministry has consisted of debating with believers and challenging them to really look at what they're learning from Word of Faith and health and wealth preachers as well as the "purpose-driven" ideology and "me-centered" pseudo-Christianity that is modern American evangelicalism. Taking our cue from Aquila and Priscilla, who instructed Apollos in the faith, we have, however, come to understand the tool of apologetics better. Instead of just looking at the tool and admiring it in our own toolbox, we were instructed in its proper use and qualified to use it in greater strength than before because we learned the inner workings of this great, yet often neglected, tool. Then, above that, zeal began to grow to develop a cadre of believers who can use this tool, utilizing the discipline of apologetics both in polemic and irenic situations and use it efficiently and successfully.

If we are to define discernment, it is simply the ability to detect and distinguish the difference between truth and error, right and wrong. Discernment sharpens our mind to make careful distinctions about what is true and what is false. As we begin to distinguish between the two, it is really learning how to think biblically. Not only are we to know what we believe and why we believe it, but we are also to be able to "examine everything carefully." When we examine teachings carefully, we then, as Paul said, "Hold fast what is good. Abstain from every form of evil" (cf. 1 Thess 5:21–22).

John warned us that we were not to take everything at face value, but we are to "test the spirits to see whether they are from God." Why? Because we want to be judgmental and picky? No. It is because we are warned that there are many "false prophets" in the world (cf. 1 John 4:1).

What is our textbook for discernment? Believe it or not, the scriptures tell us what it is. The Bible. Second Peter 1:3–5 says:

> His divine power has granted to us all things that pertain to life and Godliness, through the knowledge of him who called us to his own glory and excellence, by which he has granted to us his precious and very great promises, so that through them you may become partakers of the divine nature, having escaped from the corruption that is in the world because of sinful desire. For this

Just a Little Discernment, Please!

very reason, make every effort to supplement your faith with virtue, and virtue with knowledge.

Everything we need with regard to our natural life and spiritual life has already been given to us. There is no need to get a "word" from the Lord or a prophetic utterance. There is no need to go to the prophetic conference and have your dream interpreted. Everything we need has been given through the knowledge of God. Where is that knowledge found? It is found exclusively in the word of God—the infallible, inspired, and inerrant word of God.

> But false prophets also arose among the people, just as there will be false teachers among you, who will secretly bring in destructive heresies, even denying the Master who bought them, bringing upon themselves swift destruction. And many will follow their sensuality, and because of them the way of truth will be blasphemed. And in their greed they will exploit you with false words. Their condemnation from long ago is not idle, and their destruction is not asleep. (2 Pet 2:1–3)

How does one know what is a destructive heresy? A false teaching? How does one not get exploited? One must study the word of God. Discernment: it is imperative for all Christians to exercise this tool, sharpening, polishing, and learning to use it properly. Otherwise they are at risk of being "tossed to and fro by the waves and carried about by every wind of doctrine" (Eph 4:14).

> Obedience? Are you now a zealous proponent of something you have not really investigated fully but only "experienced"? Examine yourself and others in your congregation to see if phenomena such as "slain in the spirit" have taken on far more importance in your life than they should.[5]

The above quote is of great importance in our day of pragmatism. We live in a post-modern world where truth is relative to the individual's experience, culture, and demographics. However, scripture is not subjective truth. In fact, it is the only source of objective truth God has given to us. We can verify teachings, doctrine, and experience by the light of the word of God because it is *inerrant, infallible, inspired,* and *uncorrupted.* Our experiences *change* from day to day and from mood to mood.

---

5. Prasch, *Slain in the Spirit: A Midrashic Perspective.*

Any experience that cannot be found in scripture cannot be verified by scripture because it is outside of the written, revealed word. Since it cannot be verified to be actual acts of God, how then do we verify it as being a "move of the Spirit"? We'd have nothing to gauge it by and that leaves us open to other moves, which may be anathema to one generation of Christians and widely accepted by a later generation. Reader, if it is not in scripture, there is no way to make absolute sure it is of God. Therefore, if we cannot verify it, then we must not teach it, practice it, or believe it; in fact, we must denounce it.

If we allow one thing to come into the Church that is not prescribed by God in his word, how do we stop other unverifiable "experiences"? We would be left to each man judging for himself whether something is right or not . . . and we know what Judges says about the results of every man deciding for himself what is right. We'd be in a bigger bog than we are now in American evangelicalism.

Take courage, though, because the word of God is established, unchangeable, and unmovable. We cannot, we dare not, base our interpretations of experiences on what the majority is doing as the majority is often, if not always, wrong. We must base our beliefs and view our experiences through the critical lens of scripture alone.

7

Protestant Indulgences with Prophets and Profiteers

50. *Sitting in gilded mansions with their yachts docked at bay and their luxury cars parked side by side, they insist that the widow must send them her last penny in order to have her prayers heard by God.*

51. *They sell modern-day indulgences, procuring for themselves wealth beyond most Fortune 500 companies while promising the poor a "heavenly lottery" system.*

52. *The seed of the word has become the almighty dollar that is now stolen from the simplest of believers.*

53. *Nowhere in the scriptures is money called a "seed" we must plant in a ministry for God to hear our prayers to supply our needs.*

54. *Modern-day Tetzels sell "appointments" with the Almighty not to gain heaven, but procure heaven on earth through the acquisition of monetary and financial gain.*

55. *This is anti-Christ, for it places a price upon the very precious promises of God which say God supplies all our needs and no believer ever has to beg for bread.*

56. *Why don't these prophets and apostles, whose wealth is today greater than the riches of the richest, sell their own luxury cars, yachts, homes, and jewels to supply for their own ministries and take the gospel to the farthest corners of the globe?*

57. *These profiteers, instead of casting the nets out and fishing for the salvation of men's souls, fish for men's wallets.*

58. *False confidence now fills the evangelical world. From the self-esteem gospel, to the health and wealth gospel, from those who have transformed the gospel into a product to be sold and sinners into consumers who want to buy, to others who treat the Christian faith as being true simply because it works.*

59. *If indeed God will bless those with abundance who give to him sacrificially, why are these hucksters not opening their vaults and pouring out from their abundance, thereby becoming recipients of the "seed faith" they put forth and by that "faith" procuring for themselves all that is needed for their ministries to reach the unreached?*

60. *Injury is done to the word of God when preachers spend the majority of time in their sermons huckstering prayer cloths, miracle water, and holy land oils that will bring blessings to the home that sends in their "tithes" instead of preaching the unadulterated gospel of Christ and the free forgiveness of sins.*

61. *Let him who preaches "seed faith" or "miracle" products be anathema.*

62. *Wicked and evil are those who promise physical healings through offerings as if God cannot heal on his own but needs our money to procure his grace.*

63. *Wicked and evil are those who tell us that if we want to receive thousands we must give hundreds.*

64. *Wicked and evil are those who sell us modern-day indulgences of healings, miracles, and prosperity while stealing from us the purity of the gospel of God, which makes one rich where moths and rust do not corrupt.*

65. *Christians are to be taught that he who sees a man in need and passes him by, giving his money as "seed faith" instead to procure a new car or pay off his debts (keeping in mind that no Christian is to owe any man anything but love) does not purchase for himself the grace of God but instead the indignation and anger of our Lord.*

66. *Christians are to be taught that offerings sent to ministries are to come from a heart of compassion and not clouded by an "if I do this, God will have to do that" mentality.*

Protestant Indulgences with Prophets and Profiteers

> 67. *Christians are to be taught that they are first to supply for their own household, then that of their local congregation, the poor and needy, and then missions. To constantly send money in to televangelists, whose budgets can be held in better stewardship, is to neglect the feeding of your own family and household of faith.*

Some may come to this chapter and think, "Indulgences? That's pretty harsh" or even, "Watch out! Do not touch the Lord's prophets..." Well, that aspect has already been dealt with. Yet, the title is appropriate when you think about the ruthless and uncaring manner in which these televangelists and preachers scam believers out of their hard-earned finances.

First, let me explain indulgences so that you understand why the same term is used against these Charismatic and Word of Faith preachers and teachers. Over five hundred years ago, a wicked and heretical teaching, similar to the prosperity teaching of today, was rampant throughout the Roman Catholic Church. The abuses of the priests prompted Martin Luther to write out his Ninety-five Theses, the format of which is the foundation of this book, and post them on the door of Castle Church at Wittenberg in Germany on October 31, 1517. A large sum of money was needed to complete the building of St. Peter's Basilica and Pope Leo X needed desperately to finance this project. He issued a Papal Decree, which guaranteed anyone who donated finances reduced time in Purgatory either for themselves personally, a family member, or a loved one.

Among the priests sent out with this papal authority was Johann Tetzel, who made his way through Germany declaring that anyone who bought an indulgence could choose a soul to get out of purgatory. The short little saying that he had went something like this, "When the coin in the coffer rings, a soul from purgatory springs."

While these indulgences of old promised salvation in exchange for a gift to the church, the indulgences of today promise a return in finances, health, or even the salvation of your relative if the right amount of money is sent to an "anointed ministry." How do you tell which one is anointed? Of course an anointed ministry is one that has been financially blessed by God. Both positions, the papal bull from Leo the Tenth and the prosperity teachings from today's televangelists, Charismatic preachers, and word of Faith preachers, are based upon the ideology that you can purchase favor from God. Luther held to the belief that God's benefits were not for sale;

that you could not buy salvation then or healing now by giving to the "church." His first thesis stated:

> Every true Christian, be he still alive or already dead, partakes in all benefits of Christ and of the Church given him by God, even without letters of indulgence.[1]

The people dealt with in this chapter promise a lot and give back nothing. In fact, this morning in my e-mail was an article about TBN's dilemma over whether they should return the finances of a mentally challenged individual.[2] The case is now in court in South Africa.

These hucksters have the audacity to use, or rather misuse, the scriptures to wrestle money out of the wallets of hundreds of thousands of people all on the premise that if they give hundreds, they will receive thousands back. If a corporation makes a guarantee for a return on an investment and the return never comes, we call that fraud. If a company makes promises about the guarantee of a product and that guarantee doesn't come through, we call that fraud. If a preacher makes a guarantee about healing or income for donations, we call that "seed faith." And if it does not come to fruition, they call it a "lack of faith."

Something is wrong when the professed Church of Christ just tolerates this. We are allowing little lambs to be fleeced and slaughtered while those of us who know better are, for the most part, silent. Unless the Body of Christ rises up and starts going after these wolves, we will be just as guilty as they are for allowing God's children to be destroyed.

These people will stoop to any level, tell any lie, falsely prophesy in our Lord's name, or declare they are writing you personally based on a divine vision or revelation. It does not matter to them as long as it will transfer dollars from the pockets of their "marks" into their bank accounts. Many of these charlatans use companies to send out their anointed "trinkets" on a regular basis.

> "And *in their greed they will exploit you* with false words. Their condemnation from long ago is not idle, and their destruction is not asleep." (2 Pet 2:3; emphasis added)

> "Have a need? Plant a seed!" According to (*name withheld*): "God himself has established the law of sowing and reaping, of giving

---

1. *Martin Luther's Theses*, # 37.

2. Scrooby, "TBN Seeks Legal Advice on Returning Ill Man's Donation," (accessed July 23, 2007).

and receiving. Under the New Covenant you can make every act of giving a seed planted which brings you into the *Seed-Faith* lifestyle of sowing and reaping which I have been led to call 'A Blessing-Pact Covenant with God.'"

This same teaching can be heard over and again on many various "Christian" television stations globally. Here it is echoed by one of the most prominent Word of Faith/Charismatic leaders today, "Ah, dear partners, as we powerfully learned during our recent Praise-a-Thon, 'If you have a need, *plant a seed*," and claim that miracle you have been praying for! And as you do, God promises to '*Pay you wages*' for helping to bring in the final harvest."[3] Now, according to Charismatic leaders, God promises to "pay" us for harvesting. This is just blasphemy. God does not pay us wages; otherwise it is no longer grace. God does promise to supply our needs, and scripture makes that clear—needs and not wants.

(*Name withheld*) teaches, "The seed of giving is the seed of faith! And the seed has to be planted *before* we can speak to our mountain of need to be removed." Further, he asserts that this is guaranteed if you have faith because God has established laws of sowing and reaping, of giving and receiving, which he calls, "A blessing-pact covenant with God." This type of teaching reduces God to a "sugar daddy"—someone we go to in times of need and seemingly bribe to do things we want. This directly opposes the teaching of Jesus, who did the will of the Father above what he wanted and submitted himself to God's ordained plan of salvation. If the only begotten Son of God submitted himself to the plans and purposes of God, even when that meant his death upon a cruel Roman cross, how dare we demand from God things that are not part of his will.

Let's look now at what these specific indulgences are and how they rob God's people of their money and the true gospel. Here are just a few more of the new Pentecostal/Charismatic and Word of Faith indulgences that are offered.

> Open this anointing oil. Do not waste a drop. The spirit of Jesus is represented by this faith oil. Make a cross on your forehead with it, then by faith, go into a room by yourself and take out any money you have and make a cross on each bill. Do this in faith for God to head your money problems. Anoint your checkbook if you have one. Believe God to multiply your money according to Luke 6:38.

---

3. Crouch, "TBN Newsletter," (accessed July 23, 2007).

> Remember James 2:20 says that faith without works is dead. Do this as an act of faith ...[4]
>
> Here is your half of the Red Christmas Candle back. I want you to melt it together with other partners' candles and relight it in the Prayer Tower as you lift up my spiritual, physical, and financial needs. I am joining my faith with your faith and the faith of the other partners here is my Christmas offering to the Lord's work.[5]
>
> The Lord is leading me to loan you my "faith handkerchief" to start a miracle in your life.[6]

Here is one of the most blasphemous "partner letters" ever sent out, in my opinion. (*Name withheld*) actually writes as if it is the Lord himself writing. Should we add this to the closed cannon of scripture? Speaking directly for God when it is not God is forbidden in the scriptures. In an earlier chapter we went over the issue of prophesying in the name of God and it not coming to pass was punishable by death. How much more does speaking new "revelation" when it is not directly from the Holy Spirit endanger the speaker to the lake of fire? Yet, these preachers constantly speak as if they are being directly inspired by the Spirit of God when in actuality they are speaking by the spirit of greed.

> For Yeah I the Lord Thy God would speak unto thee saying, thru this letter I shall direct thy steps toward the blessing you have longed for. I cannot make thee follow but I would say unto thee, Follow. As you read the words of this letter they shall be as the Holy Wind of my Spirit whispering in your ears. Yea, follow these steps which my servant shall reveal unto thee for each shall be a "spiritual step" toward thy blessing. Yeah, toward thy miracle. For this shall be the beginning of (*name inserted by computer program*)'s "Decade of Reaping."[7]

He demands the fleece, a "four-inch long fleece," be returned no later than the 29th in order for him to then send you "Bible instructions for fourteen big miracles in your life." You've got to get the feeling that Martin

---

4. Humbard, "Partner Letter," (1983).

5. Roberts, "Partner Letter Christmas 1982," (1982). This is quoted from the reply portion on the form to be sent back to Oral Roberts.

6. Popoff, "Inquiry Response Letter," (December 1997).

7. Popoff, "Prayer Partner Letter," (December 1997).

Protestant Indulgences with Prophets and Profiteers

Luther would make sure these guys were fleeced in public so that they would never shame the name of our God again.

Well, if the fleece did not work, he will send you the "prayer cloud" or "prayer cloud pencil." The list unfortunately goes on and on. Have your name placed under the city of faith by (*name withheld*), placed in the "covenant book buried in Palestine" which (*name withheld*) was to take somewhere in Palestine and bury. Then there is the "point of contact for releasing" your faith. Or how about the "Widow's Mite" where "when the power of God is moving and the anointing is flowing, every kind of miracle can take place."[8] Or would you like a "Cornmeal Miracle Packet" for the "down to the wire" needs for either you or your family. This is a "proxy" seed faith gift that you would have to sow on behalf of a loved one who might need a "cornmeal miracle" harvest in his or her life.

Some may say that the preachers do not teach that these "indulgences" are for salvation. However, let us read what the president and founder of TBN, the largest Christian network, really teaches:

> If you're broke, if you're at your wit's end, if you're out of a job, out of work, let me tell ya. Not only are we gonna bless the world and preach Christ to millions and multitudes around the world, but *you can be saved, yourself, by planting seed* in this fertile soil called TBN.[9]

POINT OF CONTACT

One of the popular teachings, as described above, is the "point of contact" idea. This idea is simple at its base but is founded upon a "private revelation" that God gave to (*name withheld*). Read from his own teaching how he received this term:

> When I sought God for the [meaning of] the term point of contact, I received these words: "A point of contact is something you do and when you do it, you release your faith to God and expect to receive your miracle." In my estimation, more sick people have received their healing through using a point of contact than by any other means through my ministry ... the answer came to me through the word of God by the Holy Spirit's revelation: God was giving them a point of contact ... I saw the reason. The light switch

---

8. Hickey, "Widow's Mite Partner Letter," (accessed 6 July 2007).
9. Crouch, *"Praise the Lord"* program on TBN.

is connected to the electric power plant, the faucet is connected to the water supply, and the key is connected to the car motor. It dawned on me that all sources of power have a point at which you make contact with them. I began to understand that Jesus, in recognizing our humanness, knew we would often need to use a point of contact to *turn our faith loose to make connection with his power*.[10]

This is the teaching that is behind all of these Protestant indulgences. You must have something to touch in order to touch God and receive your blessing. Hundreds of thousands receive letters each month from these indulgence sellers that declare an anointing on some type of product that you need to touch, pray on, sleep on, or return with your offering in order for God to move on your behalf. Preachers teach that God cannot bless you unless you step out in faith, and proof of that faith must include a substantial offering, otherwise God cannot bless you. The onus is placed upon the person to bargain from the king of kings a blessing of financial prosperity or perfect healing. If it does not occur, it's not the ministry's fault, but the lack of faith, thereby causing guilt and anguish in the child of God. These charlatans must answer for their fleecing the sheep and the sheep must be warned.

The best of all these indulgence trinkets is probably the miracle picture of a prophet of God. According to a famous prosperity teacher, Jesus told him to take a picture of his son and himself and send it to all their partners so this "become the point of contact" for them in order to "loose their faith." Partners were to "hold it over the prayer sheet and your Seed-Faith gift so that the shadow of the picture covers the entire sheet."[11]

Another heretical group sent out a piece of textured paper that was supposed to be an "anointed handkerchief." Then, using Acts 19:11–12 (completely out of context, of course), they claim that this "faith handkerchief" is just like "an anointed prophet of God coming to your house to bless you." If you will only write your needs on the "prayer handkerchief" and mail it back to the "church," then all of your desires will be answered!

---

10. Roberts, Oral Roberts, *Holy Bible*, 63. *Point of Contac*. Excerpt taken from Master's Healing Presence Bible. (italics mine)

11. Hanegraaff, *Counterfeit Revival*, 204. Citing Oral and Richard Roberts, direct-mail letter, 2–3.

Over and over we are told that we need these anointed preachers and their Protestant icons in order to procure the blessings of God, which in their minds include financial prosperity and perfect health. The Church is once again being offered indulgences in order to receive the benefits of redemption. Christ procured for us all the necessary benefits for our lives; peace with God, justification by faith, imputed righteousness, and glorification when we are brought into the presence of God either at Christ's return or our death. All things that are necessary for life and godliness we already have, not through points of contact or special anointed pieces of paper that are supposed to represent faith handkerchiefs, but through the only begotten Son, our Lord and Savior Jesus Christ.

> I am astonished that you are so quickly deserting him who called you in the grace of Christ and are turning to a different gospel—not that there is another one, but there are some who trouble you and want to distort the gospel of Christ. But even if we or an angel from heaven should preach to you a gospel contrary to the one we preached to you, let him be accursed. (Gal 1:6–8)

We've bought the books, watched their Praise-a-Thons, sent in our seed money, claimed our healings, and received our prophecies and "words" from the Lord, while we never noticed the shackles close around our ankles and the chains bolt us to dark prison cells of self-worship and man-centered salvation. We listen to these men and women barking their orders at God and demanding prosperity and popularity while all the while stealing not only our money through "offerings" but also our souls through deception.

As theses fifty-six, fifty-seven, and fifty-nine stated:

- *Why don't these prophets and apostles, whose wealth is today greater than the riches of the richest, sell their own luxury cars, yachts, homes, and jewels to supply for their own ministries and take the gospel to the farthest corners of the globe?*
- *These profiteers, instead of casting the nets out and fishing for the salvation of men's souls, fish for men's wallets.*
- *If indeed God will bless those with abundance who give to him sacrificially, why are these hucksters not opening their vaults and pouring out from their abundance, thereby becoming recipients of the "seed faith" they put forth and by that "faith" procuring for*

A Modern Ninety-Five

themselves all that is needed for their ministries to reach the unreached?

As in the days of Martin Luther, the religious elite live in the lap of luxury at the expense of the people. The seed faith teaching is a heretical doctrine that is used to procure financial luxuries to satisfy the greed within. Their call to send in "your hundreds to receive thousands" plays on a basic need in most humans—financial security. But while you are sending in your "seed" to spread the gospel throughout the world, these preachers are pocketing a pretty hefty amount.

From Forbes's list of salaries, it should not surprise us that the owners and operators of TBN make over $770,000 between them. That means they are making almost $7,000 per day while asking for your gift of $10.00 because their ministry needs it. This gives a whole new meaning to the prayer, "Lord, give us our daily bread." Aside from this income, they live in a five million-dollar mansion that has nine bathrooms, an elevator, a six-car garage, a tennis court, and a pool with fountain. Hard to think that Paul, who was beaten several times, lowered in a basket down the walls of a city, shipwrecked, and stoned on various occasions, would have lived in a house like this. Look at the apostle's teaching on how servants should work and live:

> Here for the third time I am ready to come to you. And I will not be a burden, for I seek not what is yours but you. (2 Cor 12:14)

It seems that what is spewed from the televangelists is primarily their request for your possessions so that they may stockpile their own. But let us continue reading from 2 Corinthians 12:14–15, "For children are not obligated to save up for their parents, but parents for their children. I will most gladly spend and be spent for your souls. If I love you more, am I to be loved less?" The Bible also says, "For you remember, brothers, our labor and toil: we worked night and day, that we might not be a burden to any of you, while we proclaimed to you the gospel of God" (1 Thess 2:9).

Unfortunately, these are not the only ministries with outlandish salaries. To my amazement and dismay, Forbes weighed in on other prominent preachers with salaries ranging from $200,512 for a popular southern Baptist preacher to $451,707 for someone *Time Magazine* called the Protestant Pope. Of course ministers who preach the seed faith would be expected to garner a large chunk of your hard-earned money, but those who are supposed to be reaching the less fortunate with compassion making the same amounts, and in some cases even more, should alarm us.

> "We are selling Jesus. We are selling the King of kings and Lord of lords ... we are selling him ..."
>
> —Donny Swaggert,
> the son of a famous, or rather infamous, televangelist

How, then, are Christians to be good stewards for the Lord? First, as Christians we must recognize that we are no longer slaves to sin but now slaves to righteousness. All that we do must line up with righteousness and especially in these days of greed and prosperity, our spending and giving habits should glorify God. The Shorter Catechism's first question reminds us that our chief end is to glorify God and enjoy him forever. The first part deals with life here and the second the one to come. As believers we are to use, whether from our poverty or abundance, our resources for the Lord's service. What we have is not our own but is given by the Father's hand of love. Providentially he sends us seasons of fruitfulness and at times of famine. Both are to be recognized as coming from our Father's hand.

As believers, we are to care for our families. Men are to labor so that they can support their wives and children first. Second, we are to care for the one who is shepherding us, teaching us, admonishing us, encouraging us, and whose labor has been given by the Lord Jesus to pastor his sheep. We are to give to our pastor and the church we attend faithfully from our labors. Paul reminded us that we are not to muzzle the ox that treads out the grain. As a pastor's wife, I see the intensive labor my husband goes through each week, first feeding on the word through sermons and commentaries from other ministers and then studying the text for Sunday's sermon all week long. Daily he studies so that when he stands in the pulpit and delivers God's word to the congregation, he rightly divides the word, explains it, and exegetes it so that we can understand it better. Then, having been exhorted, corrected, reproved, and built up in our most holy faith, we are better equipped to live out our lives of faith. Too often those who labor intensely all week in preparation for Sunday are only seen to be working for that one or two hours on a Sunday morning. Congregations must learn that what they are fed on Sunday has been tread out all week long—studied, prayed about and prayed over, studied again, questioned, and prayed for again.

Then, as Paul teaches, we are to lay aside each week a portion to give to missions, for the laborers in the field are worthy of their hire too. Many times missionaries come to our churches and we give a dollar or two, whatever is floating at the bottom of our purses, instead of sacrificially for the building of God's Kingdom. Yet, these same people, as they watch the televangelists promise them $1,000 if they give only $100, run to their credit cards to ensure their financial blessing while placing themselves further in debt with the creditors, thinking somehow they can bribe God into giving them money, healing, or even, sad to say, salvation. When you give to these heretics and hucksters, you are blaspheming the Lord and robbing God.

It is as it was in the days of the Roman Catholic indulgences, which still continue in the form of Mass cards for which a $25.00 offering will guarantee novenas to be said on behalf of your loved one(s) to get them out of purgatory. Therefore on Christian television, you are robbed of your finances and God is robbed of his glory. He is not some heavenly slot machine into which you put $10 and hope to get back millions. He is not a "genie in the bottle" God that you can rub just the right way, "in faith" of course, so that he will grant your every desire. Lies! Lies! Lies! All from the pit of hell and proclaimed from "pulpit criminals," as James White calls them in his book *Pulpit Crimes*.

It should not surprise anyone that this is one of the fastest-growing movements within Christendom. After all, nothing will attract average people more than the promise to make them healthy and wealthy. The Word of Faith leadership knows this teaching quite well, and they are skilled in using this wicked tool quite skillfully in fleecing innocent and untrained sheep so that they do not even realize all their wool is gone and they are left naked and bare before God. Prominently on the broadcasting networks you will hear such shameless teachings as:

> Being poor is a sin, when God promises prosperity. New House? New car? That's chicken feed. That's nothing compared to what God wants to do for you.[12]

Or:

> If you've got one-dollar faith and you ask for ten thousand dollar items, it ain't going to work. It won't work. Jesus said, "According to your (faith)"; not according to God's will for you, in his own

12. MacArthur, *Charismatic Chaos*, 285.

good time, if it's according to his will, if he can work it into his busy schedule. He said, "According to your faith, be it unto you ..."[13]

There is an old book called *Pigs in the Parlor* written by a Pentecostal that has to do with demons in the Church. However, I think there should be a re-writing of that title, because we now have *"Pigs in the Pulpit"* disseminating the doctrines of demons amongst God's people who fall for it time and again, hook, line, and sinker.

Again, a good look at what scripture teaches us and warns us about is always the right thing to do:

> I appeal to you, brothers, to watch out for those who cause divisions and *create obstacles contrary to the doctrine that you have been taught*; avoid them. For such persons do not serve our Lord Christ, but their own appetites, and by smooth talk and flattery they deceive the hearts of the naive. (Rom 16:17–18)

> But false prophets also arose among the people, just as *there will be false teachers among you, who will secretly bring in destructive heresies,* even denying the Master who bought them, bringing upon themselves swift destruction. And many will follow their sensuality, and because of them the way of truth will be blasphemed. And *in their greed they will exploit you with false words*. Their condemnation from long ago is not idle, and their destruction is not asleep. (2 Pet 2:1–3; emphasis added)

> Now there is great gain in godliness with contentment, for we brought nothing into the world, and we cannot take anything out of the world. But if we have food and clothing, with these we will be content. *But those who desire to be rich fall into temptation, into a snare, into many senseless and harmful desires that plunge people into ruin and destruction. For the love of money is a root of all kinds of evils. It is through this craving that some have wandered away from the faith and pierced themselves with many pangs*. But as for you, O man of God, flee these things. Pursue righteousness, Godliness, faith, love, steadfastness, gentleness. (1 Tim 6:6–11; emphasis added)

With these scriptures before us, it behooves us to recognize that these teachings are not only in error, but they are also destructive, harmful, and contrary to the word of God. It is best to avoid these heretics altogether

---

13. Ibid., 286

8

Another Gospel: "You Too Can Be Gods" and Other Assorted Heresies

68. *Still others say, "Just speak it into existence." As if you are God. Thereby, by their own words, they are condemned, for they believe the lie of Satan, "you shall be as gods . . ."*

69. *According to modern-day "apostles," God's sovereignty now bows to man's will.*

70. *Prayer is denied and in its place is put a "claim-it" mentality demanding material goods from God as if he is some magical "genie in the bottle" God.*

71. *Oneness Pentecostals are held as brothers in Christ though they deny the Christ of the Bible.*

72. *Division is more of a concern than warning those who deny the Deity of Jesus.*

What do you need? Start creating it. Start speaking about it. Start speaking it into being. Speak to your billfold. Say, "You big, thick billfold full of money." Speak to your checkbook. Say, "You checkbook, you. You've never been so prosperous since I owned you. You're just jammed full of money."[1]

Words are containers for power they carry—creative or destructive power, positive or negative power—so we need to be speaking right things over our lives and about our futures if we expect

---

1. Hanegraaff, *Christianity in Crisis*, 351. Referencing Marilyn Hickey's prosperity teachings.

Another Gospel

to have good things happen, because what you say then is what you probably end up having tomorrow.[2]

One pastor who leads a church that recently moved into a sports arena says, "Sometimes it is hard for us to grasp that God wants us to prosper in every way ... God wants us to prosper financially, to have plenty of money, to fulfill the destiny he has laid out for us. One of the most important biblical principles which show us how to prosper is the principle of sowing and reaping. People tell me, 'He is God. If he wants to bless me, he can.' Friend, God works by laws. You can't expect to reap a harvest without first planting your seeds. If you will be faithful and do what God is asking you to do, God will do his part. Do not let the enemy deceive you into holding on to your seed; get it into the ground."[3]

Of course "the ground" is his ministry which has the "anointing" and is "blessed by God." After all, look how rich he is. You can't help but catch that these cries from the televangelists to "plant your seed" is a blatant call for your money. When will the Church wake up? Has it occurred to any, except a few small groups the televangelists love to label as "heresy hunters," that if these ministries would just speak to their own bank accounts, which contain hundreds of thousands and more likely millions of dollars, that God can give them for their million possibly a billion? But that's not how it works. You must "activate" your faith and plant your "seed" into their "anointed ministry" or purchase this "anointed CD ... book ... calendar ... wall hanging ... oil from the Holy Land ... chip of wood ... candle ... cornmeal ..." or whatever trinket is going to be given to you as a "gift" for your "gift." Beloved, these trinkets can be purchased online for pennies and you think they have some special "anointing"? How we have travelled back to Rome in so many ways ... but that's for another chapter.

The woman "prophet" quoted at the beginning of this chapter is not the only one who believes that you can "speak things into existence." A very popular woman preacher, known internationally, states in her book *The Name, the Word, the Blood* (pg. 37), "Words are containers for power." Many within the New Apostolic Reformation also push this teaching that "Words are powerful." Word Faith teachers along with the New Apostolic Reformation proponents advocate that through speaking and positive

---

2. Meyer, During Interview on *Bible Answer Man*, (accessed 16 August 2007).
3. Osteen, Letter from his ministry, 2005, (accessed August 27, 2007).

confession we can create our own reality. We can, in essence, change our destiny.

The theory goes like this: if we have been created in the image of God, then we are little gods. If God created out of nothing (ex nihilo) and we are little gods, then we too can create things just by speaking it out.

We must release our "faith-filled" words, just as God released his faith, and change our world, community, family, or whatever our little hearts desire. Much of this within the New Apostolic Reformation movement is no longer called "positive confession" but you are now taught to "declare" things in the heavenlies and only then can God activate the angels to do what you have commanded.

According to both the New Apostolic Reformation and Word of Faith/Charismatic camp, God dances to man's tune as man manipulates the spiritual laws of the universe to have whatever he wants. Oh, they will make it very pietistic by saying "We only want God's Kingdom to come" or for "people to get blessed," but their motives do not authenticate the teaching. That they believe that God cannot move on earth until we "give him permission" is blasphemous and heretical.

A foreshadow of the "declaration" teaching was what came to be known as the "name it, claim it" doctrine. This is another heretical teaching because it makes God subject to men and women. Jokingly outside and sometimes even inside Pentecostal circles this would be called "The name it, claim it, spit on it, you got it" heresy. It has been long argued that you can just name things and God would be bound to honor your "faith" and give you what you asked. One preacher admonished his congregation against praying "Your will be done" because that meant you had a lack of faith. Though scripture clearly tells us to submit our requests to God's will alone, these preachers are usurping the authority of God and demanding that he follow their will.

Several organizations have spoken out against these teachings but so far to no avail. "In brief, the teachings of the Word of Faith proponents may be summarized as follows: God created man in 'God's class' (or, as 'little gods'), with the potential to exercise the 'God kind of faith' in calling things into existence and living in prosperity and success as sovereign beings."

Now, among two of the top Word of Faith teachers, they cannot even find agreement with how this works, though both claim to have received the "formula" directly from Jesus himself during a personal visit.

Another Gospel

In the first chapter of the book entitled *Jesus Appears to Me*, the father of the Word of Faith movement claims, "The Lord Jesus Himself appeared to me. He stood within three feet of me." Then he claims he was instructed by this "Jesus" to "Write down: 1, 2, 3, 4. If anybody, anywhere, will take these four steps or put these four principles into operation, he will always receive whatever he wants from Me or from God the Father." The formula simply states this: "Say it, do it, receive it, and tell it."

Step one is "Say it." Whatever you say positively and negatively affects the universe around you. So "According to what the individual says, that shall he receive."

Step two says, "Do it." Your actions can either defeat you or help to put you over the hump. You either receive or are kept from receiving depending on what your action is.

Step three says, "Receive it." We are to plug into "the powerhouse of heaven." "Faith is the plug ... Just plug in!" This week I heard that our faith opens God's faucet and "Praise God, it'll just keep coming."

Step four says, "Tell it so others may believe." This is the Word of Faith's Evangelistic Mission Statement.

However, the hopeful successor-to-be seems to have received a direct revelation from "Jesus" that is slightly different than what Jesus told the father of the movement. His instructions are as follows.

"All it takes is 1) Seeing or visualizing whatever you need, whether physical or financial; 2) Staking your claim on scripture; and 3) Speaking it into existence."[4]

Word of Faith adherents believe that faith works like a power or force and through it we can obtain whatever we want: health, wealth, success, power, prestige, etc. But this only works through the "spoken" word because that is how our faith is released. When we speak these words, we activate our faith and power is discharged to accomplish our wishes or angels are sent to do our bidding.

One proponent says this about the tongue: "(It) can kill you, or it can release the life of God within you" because "faith is a seed ... you plant it by speaking it."

To our sinful and greedy natures, this teaching is very attractive because it means we get what we demand. We can produce our own destiny, as if God's design wasn't quite right or perfect enough, possibly having

---

4. Hanegraaff, *Christianity in Crisis*.

too much suffering or sickness or not enough health and power. We can manipulate the universe because God has set "laws" by which he is bound, and we have to learn to move within those laws by giving God permission to work and by directing the heavenlies after our own gluttonous whims.

"Now this is a shocker! But God has to be given permission to work in this earth real on behalf of man... Yes! You are in control! So if man has control, who no longer has it? God ... when God gave Adam dominion, which meant God no longer had dominion. So, God cannot do anything on this earth unless we let him or give him permission through prayer."

Another facet of this false teaching is the claim that believers are "little gods" on this earth. Since God needs our permission to move on earth and within our circumstances, it follows that we are greater than God and therefore we must be "little gods."

> *Christians are "Little Messiahs"* and "little gods" on the earth. Thus [Encouraging the audience] ... say I am a God-man. This spirit-man within me is a God-man, say I'm born of heaven a God-man. I'm a God man. I am a sample of Jesus. I'm a super being. Say it! Say it! Who's a super being? I walk in the realm of the supernatural. Say it! ... You want to prosper? Money will be falling on you from left, right, and center. God will begin to prosper you; for money always follows righteousness ... Say after me, everything I ever want is in me already.[5]

> You do not have a God in you; you are one.[6]

> That's why angels need our permission to function. It says they are here to do our bidding. They can't even act without our permission, you see. But, here's the bigger statement: Even God himself is illegal on earth. Why? Because, he is a spirit and the law he set up by his own mouth was that only spirits with bodies can function on earth legally.[7]

> So, even though God can do anything, he can only do what you permit him to do. If you study the word of God, you will see why it makes so much sense. For example, God has done nothing on

---

5. Hinn, "Benny Hinn: Apologetics Research Resources," (accessed August 15, 2007). Source: Benny Hinn on the Trinity Broadcasting Network, Dec. 6, 1990.

6. Copeland, *The Force of Love* (Tape 02-0028; n.p.: Believer's Voice of Victory, n.d.).

7. Munroe, *This is Your Day Broadcast* (Benny Hinn Ministries, Inc., 7/13/2004).

earth without a human co-operating with him. He had to find a human."[8]

But the serpent said to the woman, "You will not surely die. For God knows that when you eat of it your eyes will be opened, and you will be like God, knowing good and evil." (Gen 3:4–5)

"You will be like God . . ." Too many preachers and teachers have succumbed to this deception and propagate it to their congregations thereby multiplying the lie exponentially. So down throughout the ages, since Satan's discussion with Eve, men and women everywhere have desired to "be like God."

Often, this teaching was relegated to New Age lies. Unfortunately, however, the Church has picked up this lie and has run with it. Today, as you listen to preachers on "Christian television," you will be told the lies that God needs your permission to move on earth and within your circumstances. You will be told that you have "creative power" in your tongue. You will be told that you can demand things from God because it is your "right" as a child of God to have "heaven on earth."[9] All these are variations of the lie that Satan told Eve on that fateful day when mankind fell into sin, "You will be like God . . ."

THE SCRIPTURE'S RESPONSE

Again, it cannot be emphasized enough that one must always evaluate teachings and doctrine from the scriptures. So, let us now look at what the Bible says about the sovereignty of God and his power and control over creation. From the Westminster Confession of Faith we read:

> 3:1 God from all eternity did, by the most wise and holy counsel of His own will, freely, and unchangeably ordain whatsoever comes to pass. (Rom 9:15, 18; 11:33; Eph 1:11; Heb 6:17)

> For he says to Moses, "I will have mercy on whom I have mercy, and I will have compassion on whom I have compassion." (Rom 9:15)

> So then he has mercy on whomever he wills, and he hardens whomever he wills. (Rom 9:18)

---

8. Ibid.
9. Lehman, July 31, 2007—Blue Mountain Christian Retreat Center Evening Session.

> Oh, the depth of the riches and wisdom and knowledge of God! How unsearchable are his judgments and how inscrutable his ways. (Rom 11:33)
>
> In him we have obtained an inheritance, having been predestined according to the purpose of him who works all things according to the counsel of his will. (Eph 1:11)
>
> So when God desired to show more convincingly to the heirs of the promise the unchangeable character of his purpose, he guaranteed it with an oath. (Heb 6:17)

In the above passages from God's word, which we have already established to be authoritative, inspired, infallible, and inerrant, we come to understand the sovereignty of God over all things. From who will be saved, through the elective grace of God, to the control of the smallest thing such as the roll of dice (cf. Prov 16:33), all things are under the sovereign control of the blessed, triune God. In fact, all things "come to us not by chance but from his Fatherly Hand" (Catechism 1561).

Christians are to be taught that the Lord rules everything he has created and still upholds and rules them through providence and his eternal decrees. He is the only one with creative power over his creation and all his will comes to pass. He is the only one, as God alone, who can create out of nothing. He is the sovereign Lord of heaven and earth and that is why when we approach him we open our prayers with "Our Heavenly Father." This is to remind us that he is Lord of the universe, the only God and beside him there is no other.

Yet, the Charismatics and Word of Faith adherents would have us believe that we too are little gods. Do they not recognize the similarity of that thought with the teaching of the Mormon Church, which advocates that mortal men can become gods who will rule over their own planets? A little studying of the scriptures would make this plain even to the simplest of persons.

The Westminster Shorter Catechism states this:

> *Question 7.* What are the decrees of God?
>
> *Answer.* The decrees of God are his eternal purpose according to the counsel of his will, whereby, for his own glory, he hath foreordained whatsoever comes to pass.

When we pray, we were instructed by Jesus himself to pray, "Thy will be done." Yet, these usurpers would deny the very words of their Lord and instead teach doctrines of demons (cf. Jude 4). Further scripture warns us to avoid those who twist the word of God:

> If anyone teaches a different doctrine and does not agree with the sound words of our Lord Jesus Christ and the teaching that accords with godliness, he is puffed up with conceit and understands nothing. He has an unhealthy craving for controversy and for quarrels about words, which produce envy, dissension, slander, evil suspicions, and constant friction among people who are depraved in mind and deprived of the truth, imagining that godliness is a means of gain. (1 Tim 6:3–5)

Paul, through the Holy Spirit taught us what we are to pray for.

> And so, from the day we heard, we have not ceased to pray for you, asking that you may be filled with the knowledge of his will in all spiritual wisdom and understanding. (Col 1:9)

> To this end we always pray for you, that our God may make you worthy of his calling and may fulfill every resolve for good and every work of faith by his power. (2 Thess 1:11)

> For this reason, because I have heard of your faith in the Lord Jesus and your love toward all the saints, I do not cease to give thanks for you, remembering you in my prayers, that the God of our Lord Jesus Christ, the Father of glory, may give you a spirit of wisdom and of revelation in the knowledge of him, having the eyes of your hearts enlightened, that you may know what is the hope to which he has called you, what are the riches of his glorious inheritance in the saints, and what is the immeasurable greatness of his power toward us who believe, according to the working of his great might that he worked in Christ when he raised him from the dead and seated him at his right hand in the heavenly places, far above all rule and authority and power and dominion, and above every name that is named, not only in this age but also in the one to come. (Eph 1:15–21)

In not one of the above examples do we read words such as "I declare," "I claim," "I decree," or "My will be done." No. These prayers, from which we are to learn how to pray properly, all speak of growing in the grace and knowledge of our Lord and Savior.

A Modern Ninety-Five

Let us then be willing to recognize where we have erred from the word of God and repent in humility, seeking the grace of the Lord Jesus that he may be merciful to us and restore us to the true faith, which is a gift from God through which we are made acceptable to the Father through the justification found in Jesus Christ and his life, death, and resurrection.

ONENESS AND ONENESS PENTECOSTALS

In the folds of *Time Magazine* are the picture and a short blurb on a man the non-Christian world believes to be an "evangelical." The blurb states, "A master of pop psychology, *this pastor*, 47, represents a new wrinkle for evangelicals, the neo-Pentecostals, who combine intense spirituality with a therapeutic approach."[10] Though it may be well and good for the unbeliever and unregenerate to make this mistake, the danger begins when the so-called evangelical Church starts to follow this man, purchase his tapes, organize Bible studies, and the like. This then becomes a problem of cataclysmic proportions. This "evangelical" is, after all, a Oneness Pentecostal who denies the biblical understanding of the Trinity. Once again we see that ignorance of the creeds and Church history fosters an environment conducive to the widespread spawning and growth of heretical doctrines.

The usual description of our understanding of God goes like this:

> There is one God, eternally existent in the three persons of Father, Son, and Holy Spirit who is Creator of all things seen and unseen, infinitely perfect in love, power, and knowledge. These persons are the same in substance, equal in power and glory (Matt 28:19; 2 Cor 13:14). God as Father reigns with providential care over his universe, his creatures, and all of human history according to his sovereign purposes. (Courtesy of Monergism.com/our_faith.php)

This is what anti-Trinitarians will write to describe God:

> *God*—There is one God, Creator of all things, infinitely perfect, and eternally existing in three manifestations: Father, Son, and Holy Spirit.[11]

---

10. Bazemore/AP, "*TIME*: 25 Most Influential Evangelicals Photo Essay: T. D. Jakes," *Time Magazine*, (accessed August 16, 2007).

11. Unknown, "The Potter's House of Dallas—Belief Statement," (accessed August 16, 2007).

Another Gospel

From the United Pentecostal official website:

ONENESS OF GOD

> In distinction to the doctrine of the Trinity, the UPCI holds to a Oneness view of God. It views the Trinitarian concept of God, that of God eternally existing as three distinctive persons, as inadequate and a departure from the consistent and emphatic biblical revelation of God being one.
>
> The UPCI teaches that the one God who revealed himself in the Old Testament as Jehovah revealed himself in his Son, Jesus Christ. Thus Jesus Christ was and is God. In other words, Jesus is the one true God manifested in flesh, for in him dwells all the fullness of the Godhead bodily (John 1:1–14; 1 Tim 3:16; Col 2:9).
>
> While fully God, Jesus was also fully man, possessing a full and true humanity. He was both God and man. Moreover, the Holy Spirit is God with us and in us. Thus God is manifested as Father in creation and as the Father of the Son, in the Son for our redemption, and as the Holy Spirit in our regeneration.[12]

Oneness Pentecostal theology believes and affirms that there exists only one God. It believes and affirms the deity of Jesus and the Holy Spirit. However, Oneness theology denies the Trinity. Oneness theology denies the Trinity and teaches that God is a single person who was "*manifested as Father in creation and as the Father of the Son, in the Son for our redemption, and as the Holy Spirit in our regeneration.*"[13]

However, the doctrine of the Trinity is the teaching that there is one God who has revealed himself as three distinct, simultaneous persons of one essence, co-equal and co-eternal. The Trinity does not assert that there are three gods, but only one. The doctrine of the Trinity is that there is one God in three persons. In John 14:6, Jesus states, "I am the way, and the truth, and the life. No one comes to the Father except through me." This statement is so filled with proof of the deity of Jesus that if a Christian uses, expounds, and exegetes it properly, he or she will bring the non-Christian to that house of salvation where the choice to enter or walk away will be upon them. However, I am not advocating that apart from a monergistic work of God that person will ever walk through the door to the house of salvation, for they are still blind, deaf, dumb, and spiritually dead until God's Spirit works regeneration in them.

---

12. United Pentecostal Church International, "About Us," (accessed August 16, 2007).
13. Ibid.

When Jesus says that he is "the way," he is not merely saying that he is a sign on the road to God that says, "Go this way" or a mere prophet pointing out the way, but he is saying he is the very road and destination on that road. He is the way of salvation itself by his obedience and sacrifice and the only way to the Father.

Jesus then speaks of himself as "the truth," which means that he is truth itself. We know that God alone is truth and for Jesus to make this claim points to his co-equality with the Father. There is no truth other than Christ Jesus who is the true bread from heaven, the true water from the rock, and the true tabernacle.

Jesus then added, "... and the life ..." Apart from Jesus we do not have nor can we attain life. He is not merely speaking of new life or life eternal but of our very existence, without which we are dead. Earlier in John we read that Jesus is the eternal logos through which the world was created and all who live on it. God breathed into Adam and he became a living soul (cf. Gen 2:7). Jesus is stating that he is the very life of all the elect and apart from him we die. Here we see Jesus teaching that he is the very life-giving God of the universe and all that was created and all who live and breathe do so because he is life.

In the phrase, "No one comes to the Father except through him," Jesus points out that there is no other way, there is no other truth, and there is no life apart from him for the elect. If we are to come to the Father, to know God, we must travel through the one who is the road to the Father, who speaks the truth about the Father and embodies in truth all the shadows and types of the Old Testament, and by whom we are given life and a new birth so that we may know God, which is life eternal (cf. John 17:3).

In dealing with God as revealed in the scriptures, we find that we have three distinct persons mentioned—Father, Son, and Holy Spirit—but also that there is one God. This brings with it some confusion that even the most brilliant theologians cannot fully explain in a satisfactory sense. The doctrine of the Trinity is valuable because it enables us to reconcile the problem of one and the many. The word "trinity" does not appear in the Bible, yet the absence of the term does not refute the idea behind it. It is, as Benjamin Warfield states, a revealed doctrine.

> In point of fact, the doctrine of the Trinity is purely a revealed doctrine. That is to say, it embodies a truth which has never been discovered, and is indiscoverable, by natural reason. With all his searching, man has not been able to find out for himself the deep-

est things of God. Accordingly, ethnic thought has never attained a Trinitarian conception of God, nor does any ethnic religion present in its representations of the Divine Being any analogy to the doctrine of the Trinity.[14]

Therefore, one cannot be convinced of this doctrine simply in philosophical terms, nor in scientific language; it must be revealed to the individual and that only by God.

For the Christian, however, in defending the faith, the doctrine of the Trinity enables us to deal with the one and many problem. When we understand that God is omnipresent and immanent, that he is eternal and everlasting so that even the heavens cannot contain him, these attributes automatically negate there being two gods of such equality. To then say that there are two gods who have these qualities simply cannot be, for both cannot fill the whole earth at the same time without some room being necessary for the other who would fill the whole earth as well.

> This same God is revealed to us by his attributes, works, names, and words. Reason thus collaborates with revelation, for if God is eternal, then any God that is not eternal is not God. If God is immense there is necessarily room for only one God ("Do I not fill heaven and earth?").[15]

As we look upon God's omnipotence, we recognize that two cannot both possess all power, for then neither truly possesses it "all." If there is more than one God, then the faithfulness of us creatures would be separated; humans would not be able to love a number of gods with all their hearts and all of their souls and all of their minds, for scripture reminds us that we cannot serve two masters (cf. Matt 6:24).

So the teaching of the Bible that there are three distinct yet equal persons within the Godhead is the only one that is logical. Each is God, and yet we do not serve three gods but one. Each is eternal, everlasting, omnipotent, immanent, omnipresent, and all the other attributes pertaining to deity, and yet there is unity in the plurality.

---

14. Warfield, *The Works of Benjamin B. Warfield, Vol. 2*, 133.
15. Mizzi, "Truth for Today: Three Persons; One God," (accessed May 17, 2006).

9

Doctrine Matters: The True Gospel

73. *Enough! Jesus is sufficient. He took the punishment upon himself and bore the judgment due sinners.*

74. *Christians are to be taught to search the scriptures and see if what is being taught as Christianity is indeed biblical and accurate.*

75. *Love and unity are primary articles taught from pulpits, negating the responsibility of all preachers to preach the law and gospel at every opportunity, for the gospel is the power of God unto salvation.*

76. *We are commanded to preach "peace, peace" when there are ravenous wolves among us. But I daresay if there is a wolf in the sheep pen, you are not about to befriend it but get out your double-barrel shotgun and shoot it—maybe not to kill, but at least to put the fear of God into it.*

77. *Preachers declare to those dead in sins that they can raise themselves and come to Christ, denying that salvation is by grace alone through faith alone and that apart from the irresistible power of God none would come to him.*

78. *Christians are to be taught that human beings are born spiritually dead and are incapable even of cooperating with regenerating grace.*

79. *Grace and truth are what we are commanded by scripture to teach and preach.*

80. *Christians are to be taught from the word of God about Christ and his sacrificial death upon the cross, which has once and for all satis-*

fied the holy and just law of God, procuring the eternal salvation of those who truly believe and repent.

81. Scripture tells us to "pray without ceasing" and that "the effective fervent prayer of a righteous man avails much."

There are primarily two views of mankind: wounded and dead, or rather the biblical and Pelagian view (also known as Calvinism and Arminianism). Ever since the dawn of time, the division has been between saving ourselves, either by our works or choice, or to be saved by grace alone. *Biblical Christianity is the only religion in the world that states that we could not do what God required and therefore he did what was necessary to accomplish our salvation himself.* All other religions, even some that claim to be Christian, base salvation on some type of human effort (e.g., coming forward at an altar call, receiving Jesus, asking Jesus into your heart, choosing God, etc.).

The religions that blatantly base salvation on human effort make you do all types of works and religious deeds in order to get right with God. Even within Christian circles, the "choice" of salvation is what saves you, not an actual satisfaction of God's law through the propitiatory sacrifice of God's Son Jesus and the expiation of our guilt through his shed blood. This is known as a syncretistic religion and blends the work of man, which may in some instances just be your "faith," and the work of God for salvation. This is anti-biblical and must be called at best error and at worst heresy within the Church.

In the biblical teaching of salvation, redemption is based solely upon the elective grace of God. In *Bondage of the Will* by Martin Luther, he writes, "But if God is thus robbed of His power and wisdom in election, what will he be but just that idol, chance, under whose sway all things happen at random?"[1] The salvation of God belongs solely to him and his will and plan which he set forth in the council before time and in which was determined who among sinners the Father chose for salvation and for whom the Son would die and the Holy Spirit regenerate.

In the *Ordu Salutis* Chart (see chart in this chapter), you can clearly see the differences between the two theological ideas. The orders vary greatly and terms are defined differently between the views, therefore a timeline has been followed even if the theological issues do not corre-

---

1. Packer and Johnston, Martin Luther's *On the Bondage of the Will*. A New Translation of *De servo arbitrio*, 199.

spond in the same row. The biblical/Reformed view begins the benefits of salvation from a pre-temporal or "before creation" vantage while the Arminian view perceives the benefits of salvation beginning with prevenient grace. From here there are some similarities but there are also great theological differences. It should be noticed that the foundation of the Ordu Salutis determines the final stage of the benefits and whether they can be lost as in the Arminian view, or, as in the biblical view, are maintained by God's own preservation power.

Though there is a logical progression to the benefits of salvation, one should not necessarily be emphatic about the order with regard to some benefits, such as at what point does irresistible grace come in? Prior to, during, or after the gospel call? Also, the timing of the inward call—again, at what point does it come in? Is it prior to, during, or after the gospel call?

The following chart is a delineation of the two prominent views of the actualizing of salvation for the individual. If there is a correlating blank box next to an opposing view that is filled in, it is because that particular view differs in the order.

Doctrine Matters: The True Gospel

Two Opposing Views of the Order of Salvation (Ordu Salutis)

Theological Issue	Reformed Position (Monergism)	Theological Issue	Arminian Position (Synergism)
Pre-temporal Covenant	God the Father made a pre-temporal covenant with the eternal Son to redeem his people by effectually calling and supernaturally drawing them to him. Christ himself was chosen to be our Savior before the creation of the world and accomplishes this for his people in the last times by taking on their flesh, fulfilling the demands of the law **for them** in his life, death, and physical resurrection. The Holy Spirit is the one to apply the efficacy of the atonement and propitiation made by Christ to those who have been chosen by the Father. Psalm 110; John 6:37, 38, 44, 63–65, 15, 16, 17:2; Acts 13:48; Romans 8:29; Ephesians 1:3, 4; Hebrews 6:16–17; 10:5; 1 Peter 1:20		
Predestination	Based on God's eternal decree in Christ, which is according to his purpose and pleasure. Predestination is not based upon any foreseen event, such as the sinner choosing Christ, but on being foreknown and fore-loved by the Father. Ephesians 1:10, 11; Romans 8:29, 30; John 13:18; 2 Timothy 2:19		

A Modern Ninety-Five

Theological Issue	Reformed Position (Monergism)	Theological Issue	Arminian Position (Synergism)
Election	God has, before the foundation of the world, elected some to salvation. These are his people whom he has given to Jesus Christ. This election is not based on the works of these people or God's foreseeing that these would believe. It is based solely upon God's sovereign, electing grace and Jesus Christ's good works and perfect obedience, passive and active, having completely met the requirements of the law for the elect. Acts 13:4, 5; Ephesians 1:4–5; 2 Thessalonians 2:13; 2 Timothy 1:9; John 1:12–14		
Common Grace	The common grace of God that is bestowed upon all humanity without distinction. Various aspects of common grace include God's providential care of creation, such as the provision of rain and sunshine upon the crops of both believers and unbelievers alike. Providential restraint of sin, which holds back mankind from being as sinful as they could be and maintains within each human the Imago Dei and subsequent recognition of what is and what is not ethical. Providential blessings upon humanity such as medical and technological advances that have improved the lives and lifestyles of both the regenerate and unregenerate alike. Matthew 5:45; Romans 1:18–32	Prevenient Grace or Universal Enablement	"The divine love that surrounds all humanity and precedes any and all of our conscious impulses. This grace prompts our first wish to please God, our first glimmer of understanding concerning God's will, and our 'first slight transient conviction' of having sinned against God. God's grace also awakens in us an earnest longing for deliverance from sin and death and moves us toward repentance and faith."[2] Jeremiah 1:5; 31:3 Luke 19:10; Romans 2:4; Philippians 2:12–13

2. *The Book of Discipline of the United Methodist Church—2004*, Section 1: Our Doctrinal Heritage: Distinctive Wesleyan Emphases.

Doctrine Matters: The True Gospel

Theological Issue	Reformed Position (Monergism)	Theological Issue	Arminian Position (Synergism)
Gospel Call	An outward call, which is God's offer of grace to sinners, commanding them to come and receive Christ and his salvation. "Many are called, but few chosen" (Matt 22:14). This call shows men what they ought to do in order to gain salvation and renders them inexcusable in case of disobedience. This general call of the gospel, containing the supremacy of God, his wrath against sin, and the promise of salvation through his Son, exhorts fallen man to repent from their sins and believe in the redemption offered in Christ. John 12:37–39; 1 Corinthians 2:14	Outward Calling	The gospel is an invitation. It is an outward call, which is God's offer of grace to sinners, inviting them to come and accept of Christ and salvation. The call is to "whosoever will come" and since man's will has already been softened by prevenient grace, one can will to accept or reject the public call to repentance. Often this Soteriology leads to an "altar call" where those who want to "decide" or "choose" Jesus are invited to "come forward" and make a public "profession of faith." This act, however, does not certify an actual "possession" of Christ.
Irresistible Grace	Since it is the decreed will of God that those whom he gave to his dear Son in eternity past should be saved, he will then act in sovereign grace in such a way that the elect will find Christ irresistible. This does not mean that God forces the elect to trust in his Son but rather that he gives them life and that life sets them free to repent of their sins and to put their trust wholly in him for salvation. The dead human spirit finds the spirit of Satan irresistible and the living (born-again) human spirit finds the God of the living irresistible. Philippians 1:6; Ephesians 1:11; Romans 8:14; 1 Corinthians 6:11; 1 Peter 1:2	Resistible Grace	Since God cannot force himself upon any human without infringing upon the freedom of their will, men and women can and do resist the grace of God and so remain in their sins. Joshua 24:15

Theological Issue	Reformed Position (Monergism)	Theological Issue	Arminian Position (Synergism)
		Repentance	Man's free will is the final arbiter in his salvation. He is free to accept or reject God's "offer." Repentance is a verbal assent to the truth and does not necessarily include a change of mind and life.
Regeneration	The Holy Spirit is the only efficient agent in regeneration (monergism). Apart from regeneration, man is unwilling and unable, being dead in sins, to lift a finger toward his own salvation. Salvation is sovereignly dispensed by the Holy Spirit according to the eternal will of God (at a time of his choosing). God sends his Spirit into his elect to change this spiritual rebellion by regenerating, renewing, and transforming the inward condition of the depraved into a love for the Lord. In effect, these hearts and natures have been born again, and their eyes and ears have been opened to see the glorious truths of God's salvation. John 3:3, 7; 1 Peter 1:3, 23; Ezekiel 36:26; 2 Corinthians 5:17; Galatians 6:15	Decisional Regeneration	God works together with man in regeneration. Man's choice ultimately determines and causes God to regenerate the sinner (synergism). It is dependent on man accepting Christ, being a seeker, and responding to the gospel because he chose to do so out of his own free volition. Jesus only provided a way of salvation for us at the cross and now sits in the heavenlies waiting for lost people to seek him, choose him, find him, accept him, and "select him." We are "elected, because I selected." John 3; Matthew 7:24, 10:32

Doctrine Matters: The True Gospel

Theological Issue	Reformed Position (Monergism)	Theological Issue	Arminian Position (Synergism)
Faith	Through the preaching of the gospel, the promise of God is heard and through that the Holy Spirit grants faith. This grace of faith enables the elect to believe "to the saving of their souls" and is the work of the Holy Spirit alone through the ministry of the word. It is this faith that unites us with Christ and thereby gives to us every gift that God gives to every one of his children. It is sovereignly dispensed by the Holy Spirit according to the eternal will of God (at a time of his choosing). Romans 1:16–8, 3:22, 5:1, 10:17; Galatians 2:16; Ephesians 2:8; Philippians 3:9; Acts 16:14; Hebrews 12:25; John 6:44	Conditional Election	Election is contingent upon faith. God looks ahead, sees who will believe, elects those whom he sees will believe, and bestows grace on them. God, who transcends all time and human history, foresees those who choose Jesus and elects them unto salvation based upon their decision. Election is not the arbitrary choice of God nor based upon some hidden motive unknown to mankind; it is based upon God's foreknowledge of those who would, in time, choose to be saved. Romans 8:28–30; Mathew 10:33; Revelation 22:17
Repentance	It is sovereignly dispensed by the Holy Spirit according to the eternal will of God (at a time of his choosing). It is a gift whereby the elect reprobate is granted the ability and desire to repent and indeed does repent. Acts 26:20, 20:21; Joel 2:12–14, 3:9; Acts 3:19; Isaiah 46:8; Luke 5:32		

Theological Issue	Reformed Position (Monergism)	Theological Issue	Arminian Position (Synergism)
Justification	God's act of declaring a sinner righteous before God. Justification is instantaneous and complete, forensic, and based upon an alien righteousness (that which is outside of ourselves), which is Christ's and is imputed to us. Justification is unable to be lost since it is bound in the unity of the believer to Christ and is the judicial basis for sanctification and always leads to sanctification. It is based upon the substitutionary atonement of Christ, noting that his death paid the full penalty, once for all the sins of his people, and therefore the debt of sin is no longer on the account of the redeemed sinner but was placed on Christ on the cross wherein he actually paid the debt owed to the holiness and justice of God completely, leaving no sin unpunished for those for whom he died. Acts 16:31; Romans 3:30; 5:1; Galatians 2:16–20	Justification	Justification is defined as consisting simply of pardon of transgressions past. This justification is only purchased by Christ in this, that he procured from God the admission of a lower covenant, admitting faith and the evangelical obedience flowing out of it as righteousness in place of the perfect obedience of the covenant of works. According to the higher, our faith (without the works and its fruits) is imputed to us for righteousness, according, as they suppose, to Romans 4:5. Both deny the proper imputation of Christ's active (as distinguished from his passive) obedience and deny any imputation, except of the believer's own faith; although the higher Arminians, in making this denial, seem to misunderstand imputation as a transference of moral character.

Doctrine Matters: The True Gospel

Theological Issue	Reformed Position (Monergism)	Theological Issue	Arminian Position (Synergism)
		Contingent Predestination	Based on the foreseen faith of humans, God then predestines them to salvation. Predestination is not the predetermination of who will believe, but rather the predetermination of the believer's future inheritance. The elect are therefore predestined to sonship through adoption, glorification, and eternal life.[3] This is the fixing of a general principle that all unbelievers will perish. Romans 8:29
Sanctification	The day-to-day process by which believers are brought into conformity with the revealed will of God and live lives of greater and greater obedience. This is, in the sense of God's perspective, an act that he does and is complete, and from the human standpoint, one in which we cooperate with God addition to our faith, virtue, knowledge, etc., as St. Peter declares. No one will be perfectly sanctified while here on earth and for that reason we have an advocate who pleads before the throne of grace for forgiveness on our behalf. Acts 26:18; 1 Corinthians 1:2, 6:11; Hebrews 10:10; 1 Peter 1:5–9; 1 John 1:9–10; Jude 1:1	Christian Perfection (Wesleyan-Holiness-Pentecostal distinctives)	According to Wesley's teaching, Christians could reach perfection in this life. Christian perfection, according to Wesley, is "purity of intention, dedicating all the life to God" and "the mind which was in Christ, enabling us to walk as Christ walked." It is "loving God with all our heart, and our neighbor as ourselves."[4] Christian perfection did not imply perfection of bodily health or an infallibility of judgment. It also does not mean we no longer violate the will of God, for involuntary transgressions remain. Perfected Christians remain subject to temptation and have continued need to pray for forgiveness and holiness. It is not an absolute perfection but a perfection in love.

3. Pawson, *Once Saved, Always Saved? A Study in Perseverance and Inheritance*, 109ff.

4. Wesley, *A Plain Account of Christian Perfection*.

Theological Issue	Reformed Position (Monergism)	Theological Issue	Arminian Position (Synergism)
Perseverance or Preservation of the Saints	Those he predestined ... he also glorified. Perseverance of the elect based on God's promise. They whom God has accepted in his beloved, effectually called and sanctified by His Spirit, can neither totally, nor finally, fall away from the state of grace, but will certainly persevere therein to the end and be eternally saved This perseverance of the saints depends not upon their own free will, but upon the immutability of the decree of election flowing from the free and unchangeable love of God the Father upon the efficacy of the merit and intercession of Jesus Christ; the abiding of the Spirit and of the seed of God within them; and the nature of the covenant of grace, from which arises also the certainty and infallibility thereof.[5] Jeremiah 31:3, 32:40; Luke 22:32, 24; John 10:28, 14:16, 17:11; Romans 8:20, 33–39; 2 Thessalonians 3:3; 2 Timothy 2:18, 19; Hebrews 7:25, 9:12–15, 10:10, 14, 13:20, 21; 1 John 2:19, 27, 3:9	Perseverance of the Saints	Perseverance dependent on the obedience of man. Loss of salvation is possible. Even after accepting salvation, man is free to lose it by turning back to a life of sin. God does not make him stand, and he can have no assurance of his salvation. All believers have full assurance of salvation with the condition that they remain in Christ. Salvation is conditioned on faith, therefore perseverance is also conditioned.

5. Kelly et al., *The Westminster Confession of Faith: An Authentic Modern Version.*

Theological Issue	Reformed Position (Monergism)	Theological Issue	Arminian Position (Synergism)
Glorification	The final state for the believer wherein having already had the penalty of sin and the power of sin removed upon conversion and justification, has now been removed from the very presence of sin for all eternity. Glorification is set firmly in the eternal decrees of God through election and predestination. Romans 8:17, 28–30; Ephesians 1:11, 13; 1 John 3:24	Glorification	The final state for believers who by their consistent obedience and faith have maintained salvation to the death and wherein they are finally removed from the power, penalty, and presence of sin. Glorification is set on the continued obedience and faith of the professing believer and is guaranteed to no one, nor should it be assumed as a given for those who have placed their trust in Christ, for those who have decided for him could, theoretically decide against him at the end and thereby prove themselves unfaithful and eternally lost. Romans 8:30; Hebrews 6:6

The biblical view states that because of the Fall, man is so corrupt and rebellious against God that apart from the regenerating and effectual work of the Holy Spirit, one is unable to repent, trust in, follow, love, please, and delight in God. This has been termed *total depravity*, total inability, and spiritual death. The Bible speaks of us as spiritually dead, spiritually undescerned, blind, deaf, and with a stony (cf. Ezek 11:19, 36:26) heart.

Arminianism, on the other hand, views that though mankind is corrupt from the Fall, man's will can come alongside the restorative assistance of the Holy Spirit that God gives to all people despite the Fall, and therefore, man has the ability to cooperate with, trust in, follow, love, please, and delight in God, often called free will and human ability. So, the question that needs to be asked when understanding the gospel is "Just how depraved is the natural man?"

That's a little like asking, after a funeral, "How dead was he?" No one is only *a little* dead at his own funeral. Likewise, no one is only *a little* condemned by God because of a lesser degree of depravity. In the same way that dead is dead, depraved is depraved. And as in death, the person has no ability to taste, see, smell, hear, move, or respond, so the spiritually dead person cannot "taste and see that the Lord is good," effectively hear the gospel call, or move to respond when the call is given unless first regenerated and given new life by the Holy Spirit through the elective grace of God who then gives the person faith and repentance which are both gifts from God.

It is vital that one continues to turn to the scriptures alone to see what God has spoken concerning spiritual truths. We will do no less here. Let us see what the Spirit specifically teaches concerning the spiritual condition of every man woman and child ever conceived.

THE NATURAL MAN IS SPIRITUALLY DEAD

> And you were dead in the trespasses and sins in which you once walked, following the course of this world, following the prince of the power of the air, the spirit that is now at work in the sons of disobedience—among whom we all once lived in the passions of our flesh, carrying out the desires of the body and the mind, and were by nature children of wrath, like the rest of mankind. But God, being rich in mercy, because of the great love with which he loved us, even when we were dead in our trespasses, made us alive together with Christ—by grace you have been saved. (Eph 2:1–5)

By nature we are spiritually dead. We were dead in trespasses and sins. Try to stir the natural man to spiritual action, and you cannot do it. Lift up his hand to good works; he has no power to perform them. Try to make the feet run in the ways of righteousness; they will not move an inch. The fact is that the heart is dead.

The eye cannot perceive any beauty in Jesus Christ, nor can the nostril discover the fragrance of the Lord's sweet spices, nor can the ear hear the voice of the beloved. The man is absolutely and entirely dead as to anything with regard to spiritual life. There he lies in the grave of his corruption, and must lie there and rot too, unless divine grace shall intervene and regenerate the spirit.

THE NATURAL MAN'S HEART IS DESPERATELY WICKED

> And when the LORD smelled the pleasing aroma, the LORD said in his heart, "I will never again curse the ground because of man, for *the intention of man's heart is evil from his youth*. Neither will I

> ever again strike down every living creature as I have done. (Gen 8:21; emphasis added)

> The *heart is deceitful above all things, and desperately sick*; who can understand it? (Jer 17:9; emphasis added)

> And I will give them one heart, and a new spirit I will put within them. I will remove the *heart of stone* from their flesh and give them a heart of flesh, that they may walk in my statutes and keep my rules and obey them. And they shall be my people, and I will be their God. (Ezek 11:19–20; emphasis added)

> And I will give you a new heart, and a new spirit I will put within you. And I will remove the *heart of stone* from your flesh and give you a heart of flesh. And I will put my Spirit within you, and cause you to walk in my statutes and be careful to obey my rules. (Ezek 36:26–27; emphasis added)

> But this is the covenant that I will make with the house of Israel after those days, declares the LORD: I will put my law within them, and I will write it on their hearts. And I will be their God, and they shall be my people. (Jer 31:33)

No matter what someone may have taught you about the "freedom of choice" that men and women have, the Bible speaks of the exact opposite to be true. The only freedom of choice that mankind maintains is the choice to choose what comes naturally; and what comes naturally to the depraved nature is sin and rebellion.

THE NATURAL MAN IS ENSLAVED BY SIN

In 1 John 5:19 we are told that, with the exception of true Christians, "the whole world lies in the power of the evil one" (NASB). To be under the power of another is to be obligated to behave according to a foreign will, as a slave is compelled to obey his master. Who, or what, holds that power over the natural man? Who is his master?

> And they may come to their senses and escape from the snare of the devil, after being captured by him to do his will. (2 Tim 2:26)

So in one sense, Satan is the master of the natural man.

THE NATURAL MAN IS IN BONDAGE TO THE DESIRES OF HIS OWN HEART

As Paul wrote to Titus, "We ourselves were once foolish, disobedient, led astray, *slaves to various passions and pleasures* . . ." (Titus 3:3; emphasis added). The responsibility for the natural man's slavery to sin cannot be laid at the feet of another. It is a willful, voluntary enslavement. This is explained nowhere more clearly than in Romans 6.

> Do you not know that to whom you present yourselves slaves to obey, you are that one's slaves whom you obey, whether of sin leading to death, or of obedience leading to righteousness? . . . For just as you presented your members as slaves of uncleanness, and of lawlessness leading to more lawlessness, so now present your members as slaves of righteousness for holiness. (Rom 6:16, 19; NKJV)

The natural man does not serve sin out of begrudging obligation when he would rather be holy. He is inclined *by nature* to love sin and hate holiness.

THE NATURAL MAN TREATS GOD AS AN ENEMY

> For the wrath of God is revealed from heaven against all ungodliness and unrighteousness of men, who suppress the truth in unrighteousness, because what may be known of God is manifest in them, for God has shown it to them. For since the creation of the world His invisible attributes are clearly seen, being understood by the things that are made, even His eternal power and Godhead, so that they are without excuse, because, although they knew God, they did not glorify Him as God, nor were thankful, but became futile in their thoughts, and their foolish hearts were darkened. Professing to be wise, they became fools, and changed the glory of the incorruptible God into an image made like corruptible man—and birds and four-footed animals and creeping things. (Rom 1:18–23; NKJV)

THE NATURAL MAN ALWAYS REJECTS THE GOSPEL OF GOD'S GRACE

No natural person ever has, or ever will, truly loved God, trusted in Christ, repented of sin, or understood the gospel.

> Most assuredly, I say to you, unless one is born again, he cannot see the kingdom of God. (John 3:3; NKJV)

> For to be carnally minded is death, but to be spiritually minded is life and peace. Because the carnal mind is enmity against God; for it is not subject to the law of God, nor indeed can be. So then, those who are in the flesh cannot please God. (Rom 8:6–8; NKJV)

> But a natural man does not accept the things of the Spirit of God, for they are foolishness to him; and he cannot understand them, because they are spiritually appraised. (1 Cor 2:14; NASB)

WHAT ABOUT "FREE WILL"?

First, when discussing "free will," one should understand the position the speaker or writer is taking regarding that phrase and how he or she is defining it. When discussing "free will," one must explain what is meant by "free." Does free mean "free from sin," "free from God's will," and/or "free from God's decrees"? If the position is taken that by the term "free" what is meant is free from external coercion, then no one is truly free. Therefore, we are not really free, for if by necessity one must choose something, then one's will is indeed coerced into that choice by said necessity. Also, if Jesus said that we are "slaves to sin" (Rom 6), then a slave is not free and therefore sin, to which we are enslaved, coerces the slave it owns to do its commands. Therefore, the biblical response is that no one is truly "free"

It is correct to state that a man has a will but it is not truly free because it is in bondage to sin and out of necessity chooses sin because that is what it is bound to. We, therefore, must define this concept biblically; mankind does not possess a free will but instead his will is in bondage to sin.

Since it is impossible for anyone not to sin, sin is inevitable. Therefore, the ability to do good or evil does not exist because of the bondage each of us is under prior to God regenerating us and granting us new birth. This is where love comes in. Isaiah the prophet said, "In His love and in His pity, He redeemed them" (Isa 63:9; NKJV). St. Paul continues this declaration of immeasurable love when he wrote to the Ephesians under the anointing of the Holy Spirit:

> But God, who is rich in mercy, because of His great love with which He loved us, even when we were dead in trespasses, made us alive together with Christ (by grace you have been saved), and

raised us up together, and made us sit together in the heavenly places in Christ Jesus, that in the ages to come He might show the exceeding riches of His grace in His kindness toward us in Christ Jesus. (Eph 2:4–7; NKJV)

And to the Romans he wrote concerning God's love, "But God shows his love for us in that while we were still sinners, Christ died for us." (Rom 5:8; NKJV)

In light of just these few scriptures, the love of God is shown to be free toward those he chooses to reveal it and upon those whom he wills to pour it out upon. Paul, by the Holy Spirit, taught us in Romans that just as the master of a house has some vessels for honorable use and others for dishonorable, so too God has specifically selected some to whom he wills to pour out his saving love upon.

The scriptures clearly teach that man's will is corrupt and therefore, only by God's decretive love can any be saved. This is echoed with beautiful articulation by the divines, who penned the Westminster Confession of Faith:

> By the decree of God, for the manifestation of his glory, some men and angels are predestinated unto everlasting life, and others foreordained to everlasting death.[6]

Indeed, in God's love for fallen humanity, who by their will continually sin, for that is what sinners do, he does what mankind cannot; he reaches out and plucks some from the very fires of hell and brings them into the alabaster halls of heaven. In following the faith of the Reformers, the scriptures make it plain and clear that men do not have "free will" in the sense that they can of their own desire and sheer force of will choose God, but that God, in his great compassion and love, regenerates men and women in every language group and nation and causes them to be willing as he himself wills them to new life in Christ Jesus.

DOES GOD DETERMINE WHO IS LOST TOO?

"Saving knowledge of God comes supernaturally . . ."[7] says the *New Dictionary of Christian Apologetics* in the article on Presuppositionalism. Only when God regenerates the spirit formerly dead in trespasses and

---

6. Kelly et al., *The Westminster Confession of Faith: An Authentic Modern Version*.
7. McGrath and Campbell-Jack, *New Dictionary of Christian Apologetics*, 577.

sins can one then believe. Calvinism holds to Augustine's doctrines of grace, which Augustine placed as Pauline theology and therefore biblical theology. "That some men are eternally damned was a traditionally orthodox and almost uncontested belief."[8] Augustine stated that "the will of God is the necessity of things..."[9] These statements are to show that the reformed teaching of what is called "double predestination" is soundly held by not only Calvin but Augustine and even Luther. Luther in his *Bondage of the Will* says:

> I am to bring into the field my own resources against "free-will." Not that I shall bring them all; who could do that in this small book, when the entire Scripture, every jot and tittle of it, stands on my side? And there is no need; for "free-will" lies vanquished and prostrate already.[10]

If one's will is fallen and not free, then one's predisposition is always toward that by which it is bound. One's presuppositions are those to which one's thoughts, logic, will, heart, and motives are bound and in this case to sinfulness. Paul teaches us that what they did know about God they have changed, and their wills desire only things anti-God (cf. Rom 1:20–28).

The Arminian view, however, leaves man the capability of willing to choose God, as if the fall were not full and total, nor the depravity of man infecting all of man. The view of the Pelagian and semi-Pelagian holds that evidence and logical debate, apart from the first and monergistic work of the Holy Spirit, can sufficiently draw a sinner to Christ. The necessary part of the work of the regenerative power of the Holy Spirit, to the semi-Pelagian, is subsequent to the person's "free-will." It is not necessary to be Calvinistic in the strict sense to hold to this viewpoint, but it is necessary to be an evangelical in the Reformation's use of the word along with being confessional in their doctrinal stance.

OF GOD'S SOVEREIGNTY

With regard to the sovereignty of God, it is once again imperative that we understand the terminology we are using in our studies. When we speak

---

8. Calvin and author, *Institutes of the Christian Religion: Embracing Almost the Whole Sum of Piety & Whatever Is Necessary to Know of the Doctrine of Salvation: A Work Most Worthy To Be Read by All Persons zealous for Piety, and Recently Published*, lvii.

9. Augustine, *On Rebuke and Grace*, iviii.

10. Luther, *The Bondage of the Will*.

of the sovereignty of God, we are stating, "Whatever the Lord pleases He does, in heaven and in earth" (Ps 135:6; NKJV). We are declaring that God "works all things after the counsel of His will" (Eph 1:11). This "all things" includes the fall of sparrows (Matt 10:29), the rolling of dice (Prov 16:33), the slaughter of his people (Ps 44:11), the decisions of kings (Prov 21:1), the failing of sight (Exod 4:11), the sickness of children (2 Sam 12:15), the loss and gain of money (1 Sam 2:7), the suffering of saints (1 Pet 4:19), the completion of travel plans (Jam 4:15), the persecution of Christians (Heb 12:4–7), the repentance of souls (2 Tim 2:25), the gift of faith (Phil 1:29), the pursuit of holiness (Phil 3:12–13), the growth of believers (Heb 6:3), the giving of life and the taking in death (1 Sam 2:6), and the crucifixion of his Son (Acts 4:27–28).

Calvin teaches us that many say God did not decree that Adam should perish for his rebellion. He continues:

> As if, indeed, that very God, who, Scripture proclaims, "does whatever he pleases" [Psalm 115:3], would have created the noblest of his creatures to an uncertain end. They say that he had free choice that he might shape his own fortune, and that God ordained nothing except to treat man according to his own deserts.[11]

The conclusion is, as Calvin put it, "dreadful indeed." Nevertheless, either God is absolutely sovereign, or he is not. We do not have the choice that God has set aside his sovereignty, as the Arminiast would have us believe, so that he does not infringe upon the will of man nor make man mere puppets, if God is sovereign. Either all creation is subservient to him, and that includes evil, or God is subservient to something. The Westminster divines also tell us:

> God from all eternity, did, by the most wise and holy counsel of His own will, freely, and unchangeably ordain whatsoever comes to pass yet so, as thereby neither is God the author of sin, nor is violence offered to the will of the creatures; nor is the liberty or contingency of second causes taken away, but rather established. (WSC III)[12]

We do not believe that God is the author of evil, yet he will use sinful man to further his purposes (e.g. crucifixion of Christ) and plans. This teaches us that there really is no problem with the sovereignty of God and

11. Battles and Ford, *Institutes of the Christian Religion*, 955.
12. Kelly et al., *The Westminster Confession of Faith: An Authentic Modern Version*.

evil in the biblical sense. There may, in the philosophical and unregenerate mind, be a contradiction, but the scriptures teach no such thing.

AGREEMENT IN SCRIPTURE:

There are three passages that have one critical word in common: the word "cannot." The word describes *inability*.

1. He *cannot* see the kingdom of God (cf. John 3:3). To you it has been given to know the mystery of the kingdom of God; but to those who are outside, all things come in parables, so that "Seeing they may see [*blepo*: to see with their eyes] and not perceive [*eido*: to perceive spiritually], and hearing they may hear [with their physical ears] and not understand [spiritually]; lest they should turn and their sins be forgiven them."

2. He *cannot* be subject to the law of God (cf. Rom 8:7). The natural man does not and *will* not submit his will to God's because he *cannot* submit his will to God's. In his natural state of enmity against God, he is unable to do so. He *cannot* submit himself to Christ as his Lord and Master, meaning he cannot truly confess Jesus as "Lord" (a necessary aspect of salvation, cf. Rom 10:9; 1 Cor 12:3).

3. He *cannot* please God (cf. Rom 8:8). The natural man is often preoccupied with morality and religious activity. In every culture, among every race of men, there have always been attempts to please false gods, or a wrong perception of the true God. But what is it that truly pleases God?

He *cannot* understand the things of the Spirit of God (cf. 1 Cor 2:14). In order to understand the meaning of this verse, we must know what Paul meant by, "The things of the Spirit." The verdict that remains is that mankind is spiritually guilty of actual sin and is actually dead in sins and trespasses, unable of his own will, volition, and ability to do anything about it.

4. Apart from the grace of God in regeneration, the natural man has no hope of God. It is those "things" that are foolishness to the natural man, and what he *cannot* understand in his natural state. What are they?

With regard to his salvation, the natural, unregenerate man possesses neither the desire nor the ability to love God, to keep his laws, to repent of sin, to trust in Christ, or to understand the gospel. Unless God intervenes, the natural man will suffer eternally in hell. Humanly speaking, no natural person could ever be saved. No matter how many opportunities he is given, no matter how wide a gate is opened before him, no matter how winsomely Christ is presented, he simply *cannot, will not* see his need. He is dead in sin, guilty, and condemned, having committed spiritual suicide in Adam.

> When God puts a new heart into man, it is not because man deserves a new heart—[it is not] because there was anything good in his nature that could have prompted God to give him a new spirit. The Lord simply gives a man a new heart because He wishes to do it; that is his only reason. "But," you say, "suppose a man cries for a new heart?" I answer, no man ever did cry for a new heart until he had got one; for the cry for a new heart proves that there is a new heart there already.[13]

Is it a message of glad tidings from heaven to make God-defying rebels at ease in their wickedness? Is it given for the purpose of assuring the pleasure-crazy young people that, providing they only "believe," there is nothing for them to fear in the future? One would certainly think so from the way in which the gospel is presented, or rather perverted, by most of the "evangelists," and the more so when we look at the lives of their "converts." Surely those with any degree of spiritual discernment must perceive that to assure such that God loves them and his Son died for them, and that a full pardon for all their sins (past, present, and future) can be obtained by simply "accepting Christ as their personal Savior" is but a casting of pearls before swine.

---

13. Spurgeon, *Spurgeon's Sermons*, Volume 5, 91.

10

Seeking Purposes or Trusting Sovereign Promises?

82. *Seeker-sensitive churches have replaced houses of worship, directing man toward man instead of toward the Lord of all.*

83. *According to Romans 3:10–18, there are none who seek God from their hearts. Though we must show love and concern for the pagans who attend worship, we must be careful not to design the worship service around their desires but around God's desires.*

84. *In the seeker-driven model, the worship service is adjusted to "meet the needs" [better called "wants"] of the unbeliever, making it "relevant" for unbelievers.*

85. *The theology behind this seeker-driven movement teaches that everyone seeks for God, and all we need to do is take obstacles out of an unbeliever's way in order for him or her to come to Christ.*

86. *Purposes have replaced the promises of God.*

87. *Man would rather listen to "purposes" which are nothing more than "law-light" instead of the promises of God because man's heart is deceitful and wicked, repressing what they know about God and preferring the God of their imaginations.*

88. *Sin is no longer called an act of cosmic treason against a holy God, as Jonathan Edwards says, but instead we relegate sins to physical addictions, thereby removing all accountability and ultimately taking away sin and its judgment by medicating it.*

89. *Feelings are the gauge by which we discern truth.*

90. *Doctrine now is a syncretistic system, a blend of mysticism, dualism, and Gnosticism that borrows generously from the teachings of the metaphysical cults.*

91. *"Deeds not creeds" is the call from today's pulpits.*

92. *Numerous translations that are in actuality paraphrases are used for doctrine and teaching when they are not true to the original manuscripts but instead are man's opinion of them.*

93. *The popularity of preachers' printed materials is the basis of testing if teachings held therein are true.*

94. *Personality tests and spiritual gifts assessments are given though they are based upon the heretical teachings of Carl Jung. The biblical model with regard to the spiritual gifts is, if not utterly and completely then partially, ignored in favor of humanistic teachings and the wisdom of man.*

SEEKER-SENSITIVE

Several years ago, when my husband and I attended a Charismatic-evangelical church, we were quickly snatched up to "serve." Serving was not new to us, as pew warming was viewed as a disease. However, what we underwent in "training" was so far off scripture that we soon began to feel very uncomfortable. The first term we heard was "seeker-sensitive." The senior pastor and his team had decided that since they had finished building the actual new sanctuary, it was to be viewed as a computer, and now they were to start filling it with the proper "software" or "servers" (not in the computer sense).

Various programs from mega-churches were perused and soon we were being trained monthly in Vision Statements, Mission Statements, and other various new techniques to make our church "seeker-sensitive" and "attractive" to unbelievers. The music was the first thing to change. Whereas on our first visit to this church there was a mixture of hymns and choruses, now there was only contemporary music. Now, I have nothing against good musicians and good music, but what we were beginning to hear was typical American dumbed-down lyrics. It was the "seven-eleven music" where there are only about seven words that you sing eleven times or more. The cross of Christ, his atoning death, and even his resurrection were removed and songs that spoke of "revival" and "rivers" and being a

Seeking Purposes or Trusting Sovereign Promises?

"friend" of God, instead of balancing that with the fact that we are slaves to God, were our usual diet of what they thought was "worship." Songs that spoke of the sovereignty of God, of our bondage to sin, or our need of a Savior from the wrath of God was replaced by us "declaring" Satan under our feet, instead of Christ's, of our "freedom" from "issues" and "addictions," and of Jesus, not so much as Lord and Master, but more as our "life-coach." Suddenly the focus became inward but not even in the old holiness/pietistic mode. These were lyrics that would attract unregenerate men and women and not offend them but entice them to "Come again." John MacArthur, in his excellent video series regarding "Pragmatism," called this the "bait and switch" technique. It was and still is.

Unfortunately, neither my husband nor I recognized it quickly enough to leave immediately. So we were processed as part of the new "software" and were soon leading the "Welcome Ministry" in which we would offer coffee and cake to newcomers to make them "feel wanted and loved." We had to be a place of "community" where the neighbors would want stay. It was approximately one year later as I began to study the book of Romans again that it struck like a good two-by-four on a stubborn mule, "God's word says, 'No one seeks him.'"

> As it is written: "None is righteous, no, not one; no one understands; no one seeks for God. All have turned aside; together they have become worthless; no one does good, not even one." "Their throat is an open grave; they use their tongues to deceive." "The venom of asps is under their lips." "Their mouth is full of curses and bitterness." "Their feet are swift to shed blood; in their paths are ruin and misery, and the way of peace they have not known." "There is no fear of God before their eyes." (Rom 3:10–18)

> When God puts a new heart into man, it is not because man deserves a new heart—[it is not] because there was anything good in his nature that could have prompted God to give him a new spirit. The Lord simply gives a man a new heart because He wishes to do it; that is his only reason. "But," you say, "suppose a man cries for a new heart?" I answer, no man ever did cry for a new heart until he had got one; for the cry for a new heart proves that there is a new heart there already.[1]

How could we not have seen it? Scripture clearly states that there is no one who seeks after him, and yet we were labeling these services

---

1. Spurgeon, *Spurgeon's Sermons*, Volume 5, 91.

as "seeker sensitive." No mention of sin, law, condemnation, and/or repentance ever flowed from the pulpit again because we did not want to offend anyone. But God's word says that the gospel *is* an offense. We began to discuss with others in leadership our concerns and were told that since the "old way" wasn't working, and we weren't filling up the eighteen hundred-seat sanctuary, the pastoral leadership had sought out programs that would work.

For those who may not know the marks of a "seeker-sensitive" church, the following should be a general guide:

1. Music and lyrics are geared toward the demographic and age of the community in which your large sanctuary has been built.

2. Lyrics should not offend anyone with the law, sin, condemnation, repentance, or sanctification.

3. Lots of dancing, stage lights, mood lighting if you can afford it, and emotion-filled calls to "worship."

4. Make sure the worship is "relevant" and "meets people's felt needs."

5. Sermons should not be about how we have broken the laws of God but should be about how Jesus wants to be our friend, self-help guru, life coach, or some other therapist to equip you to make better choice or to aid you in overcoming your poor ones and the circumstances in which you were born and over which you have no control.

6. Sermons should not be long discourses on scripture because people will become bored with that and not come again. Try to make your sermons light and add lots of humor and quip little stories. Do not forget to sprinkle in the name of Jesus for good measure, but do not talk too much about the cross because you might offend someone and he or she won't want to come back.

7. Make sure that an invitation is given at the end of the sermon to "invite Jesus" into your problems and hand them over to him and he'll save you (not from sin but from your bad job, jealous co-workers, poor neighborhood, etc.).

8. Invite new people to visit the "Welcome Center" and get the free gift waiting for them.

Seeking Purposes or Trusting Sovereign Promises?

It needs to be asked: is the Bible sufficient to convict or do we need to make "church" seem "exciting," "user-friendly," "modern," "relevant," etc.? Do we believe that God has given us all we need in this book to show them the Lord's demands and requirements as well as the one who is the satisfaction of them? Do we suppose that we have to supplement the Bible with human thinking and attractions? Do we need sociological techniques to do evangelism, pop psychology, and pop psychiatry for Christian growth, extra-biblical signs or miracles for guidance, or political tools for achieving social progress and reform?

The danger in this type of gospel presentation and service is that it is not the true gospel. The true gospel emphatically states that to "know Christ is to have eternal life." This knowledge is not based upon the subjective feelings that ebb and flow in our emotions during the day, but is based on objective facts given in scripture. Once the gospel is made to be subjective, then experience trumps truth. No longer does the Church have a yardstick to maintain doctrinal integrity because there are no "facts" to prove the validity of those teachings and one is left with merely one's opinion. The American Church takes on the postmodern view that "this is my faith" and "yours is okay too if it works for you." Once faith moves to opinion, then any person's opinion is true and the anti-intellectual is packed onto the train of post-modernism which states that there are no verifiable truths.

Secondly, the Sunday worship service is not about attracting us to the church, but about God's people worshiping God. As God moved my husband and I further into the biblical format of worship and doctrine, we began to learn that Sunday was about God and not about us. Surely we benefit from it, but men and women are not the focus, God is. Soon afterwards, God brought us to the Reformed faith, and we ended up planting a church in our neighborhood. Proper worship incorporates scripture from the Old Testament, New Testament Epistles, one of the gospels, and reading or reciting the law. Songs focus our attention away from ourselves, our trials, our struggles, and onto the Sovereign Lord of the universe from whom all blessings flow. A time of private and corporate confession with absolution reminds us that we are justified yet still sinners; *simul iustus e simul es peccator* or sinner and saint at the same time. The sermon is delivered from one of the texts that have been read and expounded upon so that we comprehend what God is telling us in his word. There is no "waiting for a word" because God has given us his word and it is faithful and true. Neither is this to be a pep talk or a lecture on our "Pepsi addictions" but a faithful expounding of God's law and grace.

The sermon should encompass the law and gospel, teaching us what we ought to do, what we should not do, and what Christ did for our salvation. The call to "repent and believe" is given in each sermon, not tagged on as an "altar call" at the end of service but for believer and unbeliever alike to repent and believe in Christ for their justification. The service culminates in the celebration of the Lord's Supper. This is a visual gospel appeal for the unbelievers who may be in the service while imparting grace to the believers enabling them to live for Christ as they are fed by him through his word and the sacraments. This is true worship; the other is strictly the tickling of the ears and entertainment.

SOLI DEO GLORIA: TO GOD ALONE BE THE GLORY

Wherever in the Church biblical authority has been lost, Christ has been displaced, the gospel has been distorted, or faith has been perverted, it has always been for one reason: our interests have displaced God's and we are doing his work in our way. The loss of God's centrality in the life of today's Church is common. It is this loss that allows us to transform worship into entertainment, gospel preaching into marketing, believing into technique, being good into feeling good about ourselves, and faithfulness into being successful. As a result, God, Christ, and the Bible have come to mean too little to us.

God does not exist to satisfy human ambitions, cravings, the appetite for consumption, or our own private spiritual interests. We must focus on God in our worship rather than the satisfaction of our personal needs. God is sovereign in worship; we are not. Our concern must be for God's Kingdom, not our own empires, popularity, or success.

Let me give you this comparison:

Seeking Purposes or Trusting Sovereign Promises?
Comparison of God-centered and Man-centered Worship[2]

Category	God-centered Worship	Man-centered Worship
Goal	Glorifying God by our worship must be our goal, our highest priority (1 Cor. 10:31). It sounds elementary, but the purpose of our corporate worship service is for our congregation to worship God. Evangelism, though important, is secondary.	Bringing people in by our worship service is the highest goal in man-centered worship. Though this seems like a noble goal, it must not be our highest goal. When worship is turned into an evangelistic tool, both worship and evangelism suffer.
Pagan-friendly vs. Seeker-driven	According to Romans 3:10–18, there are none who seek God from their hearts. Though we must show love and concern for the pagans who attend worship, we must be careful not to design the worship service around their desires but around God's desires. We must remember that the greatest obstacle for the unbeliever is his sinful heart.	In the seeker-driven model, the worship service is adjusted to "meet the needs" [better called "wants"] of the unbeliever, making it "relevant" for unbelievers. The theology behind this seeker-driven movement teaches that everyone seeks for God, and all we need to do is take obstacles out of an unbeliever's way in order for him or her to come to Christ.

---

2. Hunter, "Comparison of God-centered and Man-centered Worship," (accessed July 14, 2007). Used by permission.

Offense	The gospel is inherently offensive: the spotless Lamb of God had to undergo hell on the cross for totally depraved sinners (Rom 1:16). We must share the whole counsel of God, both the offensive and inoffensive parts (Acts 20:27). Still, we must be careful not to add our own offensiveness to the mix.	Man-centered attempts at worship invariably take out the offense of the gospel to make it more palatable for so-called seekers. Sermons lack mention of sin, hell, punishment, total depravity... A gospel of salvation has no context apart from salvation from sin by the shed blood of Christ (Acts 2:36; Heb 9:22c).
Entertainment vs. Worship	Worship is done before an audience of one. We are all the participants, and the desire is that God is pleased with our worship (Rev 5:13; Phil 2:10, 11). We stand in awe of God, and then our affections are stirred, not vice versa (Acts 2:43).	Having the goal of "bringing 'em in" as the top priority will inevitably result in turning the worship hour into an entertainment session. The focus is taken off standing in awe of God and placed, instead, on what the participant will enjoy or how he or she will feel.
Needs vs. Wants	If we focus on what man truly needs, we must understand that our greatest need is for God. When we look to God first and do things his way, the outcome will meet the deepest needs of men (Matt 6:33).	In the name of being "needs-based," the focus actually becomes on what people want. While people's shallow desires are constantly fed, the deepest needs are left unmet. This camp tends to produce rapid quantitative growth and a lack of qualitative growth.
Relevance	Certainly our desire is not to be irrelevant, but the truth of God's word must never be compromised in the name of so-called relevance.	When relevance is the measure of all things, truth is invariably sacrificed.

Human Worth	Human worth is not diminished by being God-centered. Instead, it is established. That is, when we focus on God who alone has worth in himself, and we understand that we are created in his image, this brings us great worth (2 Sam 22).	Man has no worth in and of himself, and being man-centered in one's approach to anything is ultimately futile.
Sabbath-worship	God commands us in the fourth commandment to keep the Sabbath holy. In the New Testament, the Sabbath was changed from the seventh day (Saturday) (Exod 20:8–11) to the 1st day (Sunday) (See Matthew 28:1; Luke 24:1; John 20:19; Acts 20:7; Rev. 1:10). God has given us one day in seven to rest from our worldly labors and feast on him.	Sunday morning is reserved for the "evangelistic service," and worship is scheduled for another day. Saturday nights have become popular times for services, with no stress made on the biblical command and delight of corporate Sunday worship.
Spirit & Truth	God desires worshippers who will worship him in spirit and truth. (John 4:24). We must know the majestic, holy God and our sinfulness in order to worship him rightly.	Focus is often on worshipping God "in the Spirit" with very little emphasis on truth. The problem is that worship without truth, though sincere, is sincerely unpleasing to God.

The gospel as it is preached today is not the gospel that Paul preached. It has become focused on man and his problems, hang-ups, failures, and addictions. The gospel of the Kingdom is about God's forever dealing with sin and the separation of him from his creation. Man's chief purpose is to glorify God. Nothing else matters. *All of life* is to be lived under the lordship of Christ. Every activity of the Christian is to be sanctified unto the glory of God.

As the scriptures say, "Whether, then, you eat or drink or whatever you do, do all to the glory of God" (1 Cor 10:31; NASB). "Whoever speaks, is to do so as one who is speaking the utterances of God; whoever serves is to do so as one who is serving by the strength which God supplies; so that in all things God may be glorified through Jesus Christ, to whom belongs the glory and dominion forever and ever" (1 Pet 4:11; NASB). "He has made us to be a kingdom, priests to His God and Father—to Him be the glory and the dominion forever and ever" (Rev 1:6; NASB). "Grow in the grace and knowledge of our Lord and Savior Jesus Christ. To Him be the glory, both now and to the day of eternity" (2 Pet 3:18; NASB). "To Him be the glory in the church and in Christ Jesus to all generations forever and ever" (Eph 3:21; NASB). "Blessing and glory and wisdom and thanksgiving and honor and power and might, be to our God forever and ever" (Rev 7:12; NASB). "For from Him and through Him and to Him are all things. To Him be the glory forever. Amen" (Rom 11:36; NASB).

SOLI DEO GLORIA

We reaffirm that because salvation is of God and has been accomplished by God, it is for God's glory and we must glorify him always. We must live our entire lives before the face of God, under the authority of God, and for his glory alone.

We deny that we can properly glorify God if our worship is confused with entertainment, if we neglect either law or gospel in our preaching, or if self-improvement, self-esteem, or self-fulfillment are allowed to become alternatives to the gospel.

PURPOSE DRIVEN OR PROMISE CENTERED?

The priority to looking at the process of the "purpose-driven" model is that one must look deeper into the theology and see if it is based upon actual biblical doctrines and not just principles. Purposes are important, but they are not primary. The promises found in Christ are of utmost importance, and when someone has been truly regenerated, he or she will begin to live with purpose because the Spirit enables the new man within to obey the Lord of glory. However, if purposes are spoken of as primary, they are, as Michael Horton puts it, "law light" (cf. *The Promise Driven Life, Modern Reformation Magazine*).

God has given us the gospel "formula" or "model" clearly in his word. The issue is that out of pride, men and women do not want to follow the foolish way of the Lord but want to use the enticing ways of man's wisdom, which is contrary to the way God told us to proclaim his message. We have been told to go preach the gospel for "it is the power of God unto salvation." Scripture says that we preach what is a stumbling block to Jews and an offense to Greeks. Scripture says that God chose the foolish things to confound the wise. Scripture also says that all whom the Father has chosen from before the foundation of the world, for which the Son has died and whom the Spirit regenerates, will be saved. We have a gospel to preach, not an agenda.

Unfortunately, to the seeker-sensitive and purpose-driven churches, the local church is where you bring sinners in to hear about God. However, that is confusing worship with evangelism. If you want to tell sinners about the salvation proffered by Christ, speak to the ones God has placed around you at work, those in your community, your neighbors, your family members, the shop owners and workers, and all the others that you come in contact with each day. Church is where believers gather to worship. If there are pagans (unbelievers) in the group, let them see that the focus is on God, his holiness, righteousness, and provision for salvation, and let his Spirit work in them to regenerate and give them the gift of faith through grace. Church is not a hospital for sick people; it is the living Body of Christ. It is the Church Militant, as the Reformers called it.

Many evangelicals today are actually following Søran Kierkegaard's approach to the gospel, which is an extremely subjective and anti-intellectual or hyper-objective approach to the Christian faith. With regard to a portion of today's evangelicals, there are certainly many who take this approach to defending the faith and do not even realize it. Such glib statements such as, "God said it. I believe it. That settles it for me," and "Just take it by faith," or "It's a leap of faith," are clear examples of a subjective approach to the Christian faith. From the pulpits of so-called "evangelicals" comes the call to "take it by faith" and simply "believe" rather than coming to the "knowledge of the truth."

> Aquinas said that we confuse two similar yet different human actions. We see people searching desperately for peace of mind, relief from guilt, meaning and purpose to their lives, and loving acceptance. We know that ultimately these things can only be found in God. Therefore, we conclude that since people are seeking these things they must be seeking after God. People do not seek God. They seek after the benefits that only God can give them. The sin of

fallen man is this: Man seeks the benefits of God while at the same time fleeing from God himself. We are, by nature, fugitives.[3]

OF SIN

The famous sermon by Jonathan Edwards, "Sinners in the Hands of an Angry God," though still read is more a trinket for those who want to join themselves to the Great Awakening, either in hopes of a New Awakening or the pietistic movement it helped foster. However, a sermon such as this, which tells sinners that they hang like a spider held by its thread over the flames of God's wrath, would never be tolerated in most of today's churches.

As a counselor, many clients come in with "issues" and "struggles." Most of my clients find it odd that I speak of these "issues" as "sin" and are often offended. A dear friend of mine often tells me that it doesn't surprise her that my clients may only see me once or twice. When I asked her why, she stated that "you use the Book," and they do not like that.

Having been caught up in the "past memories" craze, I am well aware of how therapists will use past issues, how a person grew up, their family situation, etc., to soften the counselees' emotions. However, most who come to my office are either in rebellion, not trusting the Lord, do not believe in his sovereignty, or are blatantly sinning. Couples have come to counseling where the women admit they were not submitting but did not care because that part of the Bible was "written two thousand years ago and isn't for today." Non-submission to those whom God has placed over you is rebellion, and scripture says rebellion is as witchcraft.

Today, people do not want to hear about sin; they want to hear about how much God loves them in their sin and won't really require that they change . . . after all, isn't it all about grace? Of course it is. However, someone who has experienced the true grace of God will not and cannot continue in his or her sin. (cf. 1 John 2:4). *"It's about doing, not believing . . ."* and *"Deeds not creeds"* are the calls from today's pulpits.

> "Deeds not creeds!" has periodically become the cry of some in the Christian community. This formula expresses the American conviction that what produces results is to be endorsed and embraced. Pragmatism is in the very air we breathe.

---

3. Sproul, *Chosen by God*, 110.

Seeking Purposes or Trusting Sovereign Promises?

But what might be an appropriate admonition for those building a road is questionable for those who seek to build the church. Prominent pulpits have been filled by pastors who have marketed Jesus of Nazareth as the One who came to make us ever more efficient and successful. With considerable skill, the listener or viewer is taken on an emotional ride which precisely parallels what our society regards as suitable religious sentiments.[4]

The first Reformation was about belief; this one's going to be about behavior ... The first one was about creeds; this one's going to be about our deeds. The first one divided the church; this time it will unify the church.[5]

The *last thing many believers need today is to go to another Bible study*. They already know far more than they are putting into practice. What they need are *serving* experiences ...[6]

BELIEF AND KNOWING

How can you believe in something unless you know what that something is? This is pretty basic philosophy, so I will not get too technical here. However, can you believe in something that you do not know about or have knowledge of? Can you behave within that belief system without first gaining understanding of what that system accepts as true? The answer to both questions is an unequivocal no! Without knowledge, you would not be able to believe or trust in something. Without understanding what you believe, behaviors cannot be aligned with that belief.

What many pragmatic teachers are proposing is to throw away the knowing and just focus on the doing. By degrading the study of scripture, they teach that practice is what matters. Yet, unless you study what scripture commands to do and warns to stay away from, how can you practice what you believe?

Jesus stated that salvation was believing, trusting, and accepting as true everything he said about himself.

---

4. Wenthe and M.Div M.A., "Introduction—The Creeds," Concordia Theological Seminary, (accessed August 17, 2007).

5. Camp, "Second Reformation Will Unify Church, Warren tells Dallas GDOP," (accessed August 2, 2007).

6. Warren, *The Purpose-driven Life*, 231.

... that whoever believes in him may have eternal life. (John 3:15; NASB)

And this is eternal life, that they know you the only true God, and Jesus Christ whom you have sent. (John 17:3)

Secondly, Jesus further illuminates salvation's truth by saying that eternal life is only for those who "know" him and the Father.

From Jesus's own words, one cannot be separated from the other. Both belief and knowing must be present in order for true salvation to have occurred. What the pragmatists and seeker-driven moguls have misunderstood is that knowledge of the truth is imperative to belief and doing evidences belief. The Reformers were not just about doctrine but also about how that doctrine lived out in the lives of the common man, woman, and child. These men and women gave their lives to the blades and flames of the Inquisition because their belief system was not only in their heads but also in their hearts and lives so much that it drove Rome crazy with anger and blood-thirst.

What believers today need are churches that expound the scriptures and not impound the Bible because they do not like particular teachings within its pages. Believers need to know what they believe about God, scripture, the deity of Christ, the personhood of the Holy Spirit, justification, the atonement, the substutionary death of Christ, penal substitution, etc.

Recently, a couple in our home church was deciding whether to move to Arizona. Their son lived there and they were close to retiring, so they asked us to check out their son's church. As I spoke with one of the associate pastors on the phone, it became evident that they were about marketing the church and not proclaiming the "whole counsel of God." The associate pastor balked at my questions with regard to justification, the Lord's Supper, and the focus of the worship and belittled our small congregation, saying that they knew they were successful because they had thousands of people each week. Unfortunately, this is the focus of too many churches in our day. Church leaders are focused on Christian consumerism—not only on what they can get as Christians, but also how many Christians can they consume in their churches. How many people can they pack into their rock-concert type of worship service? How many "decision cards" can be filled out?

Instead of the focus being upon the proclamation of the gospel, which is alone the power of God for salvation, preachers and teachers zero in on a demographic or cultural group. The church I spoke of earlier in this chapter said to me that their focus is men between twenty-five and thirty-five. That was their demographic and they were creating an atmosphere conducive to bringing them in. John MacArthur called that the bait and switch routine, and he was correct.

People are enticed into the local church for what is their felt need; single moms, young college men, and retired groups are all invited to fit into church in the small group that has been created for them. Division is the name of the game within the Church as special focus groups are created to fulfill their needs. Instead of unity within the Body of Christ you have the Solid Gold group, the Adventurers, the Ambassadors, and the Married Couples group. Each is portioned in an effort to support them where they're at. Each is segregated, thereby undermining the biblical teaching that each part is necessary and an integral part of the whole. Paul tells us that the hand is as important as the foot and the inward, unseen parts often more necessary than the outward, external ones. However, once again, the theories of modern-day preachers trump those of the Bible. The mountain of pride continues to grow amongst the proponents of the seeker-driven model of Church growth.

In order to segregate the congregation, personality tests disguised as "spiritual gift analyses" are distributed to each person. This is in order for the leadership to understand the felt needs of each demographic within their congregation and evaluate what is necessary to further their church growth agendas. Spiritual gifts, which are, according to the Bible, handed out as the Spirit sovereignly determines, are viewed as talents that can be garnered from various experiences. Personality profiles are added to the examination of congregants in order to decide what ministry they are called to serve in. Instead of relying upon the Holy Spirit and the word of God, once again men think they are smarter and wiser and can figure all this out for themselves. So, congregations are duped into taking these exams and the results run through a computer that determines what spiritual gifting each individual has.

There could be much more added to this, but it is the hope of this author that the reader, by this point in the book, has understood the concept:

- Teachings that do not line up with scripture are to be thrown out
- Ideas that place man in the position of the Holy Spirit are to be discarded
- Sermons that replace the gospel with "Pepsi addiction struggles" are to be ignored.

11

The Final Word

95. *"Christians are to be exhorted that they be diligent in following Christ, their Head, through penalties, deaths, and hell; And thus be confident of entering into heaven rather through many tribulations, than through the assurance of peace"* (from Luther's Ninety-five Theses).

> Long ago, at many times and in many ways, God spoke to our fathers by the prophets, but in these last days he has spoken to us by his Son, whom he appointed the heir of all things, through whom also he created the world. He is the radiance of the glory of God and the exact imprint of his nature, and he upholds the universe by the word of his power. After making purification for sins, he sat down at the right hand of the Majesty on high, having become as much superior to angels as the name he has inherited is more excellent than theirs. (Heb 1:1–4)

Do you remember the game show hosted by Regis Philbin? Let me give you the key question on the show, and you'll remember it quick. He would give the contestant four possible responses to a question and then when the contestant gave his pick, Regis would respond with, "Is that your final answer?" In other words, is that your final word on the subject? And, if the contestant was right, he or she would progress in the game.

In order to understand the importance of the written word, one must come to an understanding of its singularity among all other writings. A grasp of the biblical teaching of inspiration and revelation and how they differ from the Spirit's role in illumination today needs to be tightly held.

A Modern Ninety-Five

GOD SPEAKING

First, how did God speak? There were several ways God spoke in the Old Testament, such as when God promised to Eve that there would come one to crush the serpent's head and whose heel would be bruised in the process. Then God spoke to the patriarchs:

- Abraham—given the covenantal blessing through which he was told that the Messiah or the "seed" (singular, not plural) would come from him and through the "seed" all nations would be blessed.
- Isaac—that Jacob would be called and not Esau, giving us the first hint of the doctrine of sovereign election superseding man's choice in the matter of salvation.
- Jacob—the Messianic line would be from Judah.
- Moses—God spoke through him by the giving of the law and revealed, "I will raise up a prophet like you from among their brothers. And I will put my words in his mouth, and he shall speak them to all that I command him" (Deut 18:18). This has traditionally been applied as a Messianic promise and was confirmed in one of the sermons of Peter recorded in Acts 3:22.

God then revealed more and more of his plan through various prophets such as:

- David, that the Messiah should be of his house.
- Micah, that the Messiah should be born at Bethlehem.
- Isaiah, that the Messiah should be born of a virgin, as well as a suffering servant and reigning king. God began to reveal in more and more detail the coming of the Messiah.

GOD SPOKE IN VARIOUS WAYS AND THROUGH VARIOUS MEANS

God revealed himself through covenants with Adam and Eve in Genesis 3:15 that there would come one to crush the serpent's head. He also revealed himself through the covenant with Abraham and to his seed, singular, to possess the promised land. He revealed himself through the law of Moses teaching us that no one can obey the law perfectly and therefore we need someone who can act as our substitute. He revealed himself through the sacrifices, pictures, and types of what the Messiah would accomplish for us. He revealed himself through the prophets in visions and visitations by angels, all focusing on the future coming of the Messiah. God had varied ways of speaking and various people he spoke to and through, yet each would speak of one specific topic most often: the coming of the Messiah to redeem God's people.

"BUT IN THESE LAST DAYS HE HAS SPOKEN TO US BY HIS SON."

"But." What a phenomenal statement. Here we have just been told the various ways that God has spoken, *but now* we are going to hear something greater, something that takes pre-eminence and precedence over all these extraordinary ways.

These gospel days are the last times, and the gospel is the final revelation that we are to expect from God. God saved his best for last and we diminish Christ if we continue to look for revelation. This is what the cults have done. The Mormons call it the "other New testament"; scientologists have their own Bible as do the Jehovah's Witness with their "new world translation." Sadly, some today, even in evangelical circles, think that God is giving "new revelation" to them. They look at their dreams and say God is speaking to them. Or they imagine they hear voices and it is God speaking.

REASONS FOR REVELATION

Natural revelation tells us that there is a creator. Then patriarchal revelation by dreams, visions, and voices told us the lineage and covenant of the Messiah. The Mosaic revelation, in the law given and written down, told us what was expected of us and was to be a tutor for us to come and recognize our need of the Messiah. The prophetic revelation came to explain the law and give clearer understanding and discoveries of Christ. But now we must expect no new revelation but only more of the Spirit of Christ to help us better understand what is already revealed. The supremacy of the gospel revelation, which God spoke through his Son, is far above all those that came previously.

Simeon, the priest, at the circumcision of Jesus called him, "A light for revelation to the Gentiles." Paul says that he received the gospel by direct revelation of Jesus Christ (Gal 1:12). Jesus is the final, finishing revelation. Jesus is "the final word." He is the most direct revelation we will ever have, and he is the ultimate revelation.

Those who think we still need revelation today do nothing but spit upon Christ as if he is not sufficient. The beauty of the revelation through Christ is that everything from the first revelation about the one who was to come and crush the serpent's head is in total agreement with the last prophecy in Malachi that he will send his messenger before the Messiah/Servant. Nothing is contradictory with the prophetic utterances in the scriptures.

However, today on TV or on Christian radio we hear such phrases as, "I had a revelation . . ." "I had this vision . . ." or "God spoke to me and revealed . . ." When we listen to what God has revealed to these supposed and false prophets, and if we were to compare them, we would come away with a God who is no God because he's telling people contradictory things.

One says that God is doing a "new work" and raising up apostles and prophets again. Another will say that all we need are "purposes" to live by and God will give us peace and prosperity. Another says all you need to do is send in this seed offering and your miracle will be on its way. And yet another falsely prophesies, "Just speak it into existence." As if you are God and have creative power. There is no continuity in the messages from evangelical pulpits today. Instead, we are subjected to the heresies of televangelists and false prophecies from so-called seers.

Scripture tells us in our text verse that God "has spoken to us in His Son" (Heb 1:2; NASB). There is a sense of culmination and finality to this verse and this final word is at its zenith. This is the height, the peak of what God has been for four thousand years revealing up to this point. It is like the capstone being placed on the building. There is a sense of it being the end of revelation, of prophetic words being terminated, not because God does not speak any longer, but because his final word is in his Son, Jesus our Lord and Savior, and this revelation is complete and perfect.

There is no greater final authority, no more direct word, and no more accurate revelation than what we have been given in the scriptures. And we know that Paul said to the Corinthians that we know in part, we prophesy in part, and when that which is "complete" comes—the full revelation of the message of Jesus Christ (we call that the New Testament)—then prophecies will stop. And why did they stop? They stopped because Jesus is the final word. He is the final revelation from God with regard to our salvation, the way to everlasting life, and redemption.

But is the Bible the only source of special revelation? What about what prophet so and so and what he or she said to me last week? What about the "words of knowledge" that sister so and so gave me? Aren't they from the Lord? No!

The Lord God Almighty gave us his written word so that we would know what he is speaking—so that we wouldn't wonder what his will is for us. So that we wouldn't walk around not knowing what he expects of us and what he plans for us. We show absolute disrespect for God by not reading his word but instead leaving it on the shelf until Sunday or Bible study. We are privileged people because we have God's final word and we dishonor him by neglecting it so often.

Hebrews 1:1–2 tells us that in times past he spoke through prophets *but now speaks to us through his son.* That hasn't changed. In the past, before the last words of the scriptures were penned, God used prophets, kings, and even shepherds to speak his word. After Christ, God used apostles and prophets to give us the history of Jesus, to record his teachings and actions, to explain the way of salvation, and to tell us the ultimate plan of God, the mystery of the ages, which is that the Gentiles are brought into the kingdom of God through faith alone in Christ alone by grace alone and alone for God's glory. Today, in these last days, he speaks to us in his Son and those words are to be found in the Bible and nowhere else.

I wrote in the beginning of this chapter that this was the covenantal blessing that God gave to Abraham and that the blessing was to his "seed" singular, so that the entire world would be blessed through this seed. God's purpose in the covenant was to be one with his people. In establishing a covenant relationship, the Lord binds himself intimately to his people. But that closeness of relationship that God intended by the covenant cannot be achieved as long as a prophetic mediator must stand between God and the people. If we think we have to be guided by our own dreams or voices, we place ourselves as the mediator between God and man. If we think we have to go see prophet so and so or this televangelist who gets direct revelation from God, then we place them in the position that solely belongs to the Son of God and to *none other.* So long as a mediator must run from the top of the mountain to the people below, covenantal unity has not been fully realized.

Only if God himself should become the one who mediates the divine word could the oneness of fellowship intended by the covenant be fulfilled. Then the need for the intermediary work of a prophet would come to an end. This outlook on the final goal of prophetic utterance is confirmed by the testimony of the new covenant documents. The New Testament is what teaches us about our great mediator, the final prophet, and the final word.

As you have read in the text, Hebrews speaks of the finality of the prophetic revelation as it is found in Jesus Christ. Previously God spoke in many different prophetic mediators. But now, he has spoken, *with finality*, in his Son. Because the prophetic revelation has come directly through Jesus Christ, the ultimate goal of the covenant has been realized.

You may ask, "But how do I know what God is telling me?" I say, "Read his revelation. Read God's word."

Do not be running to people to tell you what God's direction for your life is. Instead, run to the scriptures. If God has spoken with finality through his Son and you do not read the words of his Son, then you will run into all types of error and heresy. You will begin looking inward at the flipping of your stomach, the sweat on your palms, or your fast beating heart for direction. But all of those are subject to error. Then you may go to someone who has a "direct" connection to God. But how do you know they are not going by the flipping of their stomach, their own sweaty palms, or their own fast heartbeat? You do not. The only sure word of prophecy that we have is the direct revelation from God that it is accurate and has stood the test of time. Scripture has shown itself that it has never been wrong.

Five hundred years ago the people of God did not have the scriptures in their own language. They had to go to the priest to find out what God required, and most priests did not have their own Bible and couldn't read it if they did. So, Tyndale began to translate this precious word into English. Mary, Queen of Scots, got wind of it and began her persecution of this faithful man. Ultimately he died at the stake, burned alive for the crime of giving England the scriptures in their mother tongue. Sadly, five hundred years later, most who claim to be Christians do not read this sacred book on a regular basis. Instead we leave it aside and head for the next conference, crusade, or miracle service. We follow voices in our head, or voices in someone else's, instead of that final voice that cried, "It is finished" on the cross of Calvary.

Tragically, we have added to God's word and distorted the message of hope and life through faith in Jesus Christ alone. We have added things to our walk that are not given to us in his word and that is because we do not read his word. God spoke and is still speaking and he speaks with finality in his Son. His Son's word is sufficient and efficient to complete in us all that he intends. The words of Jesus are God's final word.

> The brothers immediately sent Paul and Silas away by night to Berea, and when they arrived they went into the Jewish synagogue. Now these Jews were nobler than those in Thessalonica; they [the Bereans] received the word with all eagerness, *examining the Scriptures daily to see if these things were so.* (Acts 17:10–11; emphasis added)

How many of you reading this today, when the pastor, preacher, or teacher is finished giving his sermon, follow up at home researching what was taught? How many of you check to see if he remained faithful and true to what the word of God says?

The Bible honors these men and women from Berea, calling them "more noble" than those in Thessalonica. Why? Were they richer? Were they better educated? No. They were nobler because 1) they received the word with eagerness and 2) examined the scriptures to see if what Paul, the great apostle himself, was preaching lined up with the scriptures.

How many reading this right now would be called "noble"? The challenge for you is to examine the theses of this book and make sure that what has been written is in line with the word of God. Then, when you attend corporate worship services, crusades, and evangelistic events, be a noble Berean and examine everything as to whether it adheres to the written, revealed, infallible, inerrant, and unchangeable word of God.

Over the centuries millions have been martyred for the faith. During the harsh years of the Reformation period, hundreds of thousands were tortured, burned alive, flayed, and torn apart for having the scriptures in their own language, reading them, or teaching them. Men such as William Tyndale, who gave us the first English Bible, were hunted down as criminals and eventually killed. Others such as Jan Hus, Jon Wyclif, and Lady Jane Grey, who at her beheading testified of the value of the written word of God for her conversion,[1] were executed because they valued the word of God, some translating it and others simply having possession of it. The scriptures were valued above their own lives, and they willingly gave up what they could not keep simply because they loved their Lord and Savior and his word.

In the days prior to the Reformation, there was a famine of God's word amongst the people. Common, everyday believers had to go to priests and prelates in order to hear God's word. Oftentimes the word of God was so barren that the priests themselves did not read it or know it. Often chained to the pulpits, the scriptures would gather dust as priests would preach on noble themes to be sure, but not on the word of God. Myths and fairytale stories would be taught instead of careful instruction in the scriptures and the people became chained to fanciful stories just as the Bible was chained to the pulpit.

Today, with dozens of translations and various study Bibles, still there is a famine amongst God's people. Instead of careful instruction, catechism, and systematic studies, preachers give their fanciful stories of overcoming "Pepsi" addictions and the like and starve their parishioners. The word of God is chained to the basement, no longer the pulpit, and anyone studying it is accused of possessing a "religious spirit." Hidden on the shelves in homes is the most incredible, the most remarkable, and the most precious commodity a family could possess. But, instead of the Bible being taken down in the morning before school and work and read to wife and children, the family scatters to their errands, completely oblivious to the spiritual nourishment they are so desperately in need of. Once the day ends, parents occupy their children's time with nonsense, play dates, and the like, neglecting to feed their family on the word of God. Men, women, teens, and children alike are fed instead books by men that offer forty days of principles to change their attitudes, lifestyle, jobs, and peers instead of picking up the one book written by God.

---

1. Foxe, *Foxe's Book of Martyrs*, (accessed August 28, 2007). "I pray you all, good Christian people, to bear me witness, that I die a good Christian woman, and that I do look to be saved by no other mean, but only by the mercy of God in the blood of His only Son Jesus Christ: and I confess that when I did know the word of God, I neglected the same, loved myself and the world, and therefore this plague and punishment is happily and worthily happened unto me for my sins; and yet I thank God, that of His goodness He hath thus given me a time and a respite to repent." Lady Jane Grey at her execution upon the Scaffold.

The Final Word

There, on the shelf, in the draw, locked up in the closet, sits the treasure whose mines can deliver the choicest of gems and precious stones if only God's people would dig . . . just a little. Gathering dust is the one book that tells us of Jesus Christ, the Savior of his people, the redeemer, the atonement, and the sacrifice accepted by God. Instead we look to television personalities to tell us what books to read, what conferences to attend, and what seminars to take when what we really need to do is take that treasure off the shelf, blow the dust off, crack open its cover, and read the word of God for ourselves, studying to show ourselves approved workmen who rightly divide the word of truth.

As millions have given their lives over the past two millennia to maintain doctrinal integrity and purity, do not let their blood have spilled in vain by clinging to the heresies they stood against. Instead join them with your very life in knowing what you believe and why you believe it.

Come, let a new reformation take place in your heart first and then the world.

Bibliography

Alexander, J.A. *The Acts of the Apostles*. 2 Volumes. n.p.: Anson d.F. Randolph, 1857.

Alliance of Confessing Evangelicals. *Cambridge Declaration*. n.p., n.d. Book on-line. Available from http://www.albatrus.org/english/creeds/reformed/cambridge_declarationl.htm; Internet.

———. *Cambridge Declaration*. n.p.: Alliance of Confessing Evangelicals, n.d. Book on-line. Available from http://www.albatrus.org/english/creeds/reformed/cambridge_declarationl.htm; Internet.

Almodovar, Nancy A. "Princess Day Update." *Silent Cry Ministries Newsletter* (March 2004).

Alnor, Jackie. "The Alnor Report," 1/33/01. http://www.deceptioninthechurch.com/hinnalnor.html.

———. "Benny Hinn—False Prophet Extraordinaire," Cephas Ministry. http://www.cephasministry.com/evangelists_benny_hinn_false_prophet_extrordinaire.html.

Anonymous. "Authority of Scripture." [journal on-line]; available from http://www.monergism.com; Internet; accessed 15 September 2006.

Archbishop Thomas Cranmer. Founders Said. Redemption. http://www.redemptiontrec.org/Paged.html.

Bazemore/AP, John. "*TIME*: 25 Most Influential Evangelicals Photo Essay: T. D. Jakes," *Time Magazine*. http://www.time.com/time/covers/1101050207/photoessay/13.html.

Benjamin Breckinridge Warfield. *Revelation and Inspiration*. New York: Oxford University Press, 1929.

Boice, James Montgomery. *Acts: An Expositional Commentary*. Grand Rapids, Mich.: Baker Books, 1997.

———. *God & History*. Downers Grove, Ill.: InterVarsity Press, 1981.

Brenham, William. n.p., n.d.

Brown, Howard, and Rodney. "Rodney Browne Comes to NY," 1997.

Buckingham, Jamie. *Daughter of Destiny: Kathryn Kuhlman, Her Story*. Plainfield, N.J.: Logos International, 1976.

Chambers, Joseph R. *Her (name withheld) & Her Spirit Guide*. North Carolina: Paw Creek Ministries, n.d.

Camp, Ken. "Second Reformation Will Unify Church, Warren Tells Dallas GDOP," 2005. Pastors.com. http://www.pastors.com/article.asp?ArtID=8280.

Clarke, Adam. *The Holy Bible, Containing the Old and New Testaments, the Text Carefully Printed from the Most Correct Copies of the Present Authorized Translation, Including the Marginal Readings and Parallel Texts: With a Commentary and Critical Notes*

Bibliography

Designed as a Help to a Better Understanding of the Sacred Writings, new ed., with the author's final corrections. Nashville: Abingdon, 1977.

Clement, Kim. n.p., n.d.

Cloud, David. "Confusion about 'Spirit Slaying,'" May 10, 2006. Fundamental Baptist Information Service. Reprinted with permission and additional notations from author added. http://www.wayoflife.org/fbns/confusion-spiritslaying.html.

Copeland, Kenneth. "Side 1." In *Spirit Soul and Body Audio Tape # 01-0601*. n.p., 1985.

———. *The Force of Love*. Tape 02-0028; n.p.: Believer's Voice of Victory, n.d.

Crouch, Paul. *"Praise the Lord"* program on TBN. n.p., n.d.

———. "TBN Newsletter," June, 2005. Trinity Broadcasting Network/Praise the Lord. http://www.tbn.org/about/newsletter/index.php/638.html.

Dabney, Robert L. *Discussions: Evangelical and Theological*. 2 Volumes. Edinburgh: Banner of Truth, 1967 (reprint 1891).

Duplantis, Jesse. *Heaven: Close Encounters of the God Kind*. Tulsa, Oklahoma: Harrison House, n.d.

Eckhardt, John. "Mobilizing the Prophetic Office." *National School of the Prophets*, Session 12 (Friday, 5/12/00, 7pm).

———. *Moving in the Apostolic*. Ventura, Calif.: Renew, 1999.

Freed, Sandie. *Get the Anointing Out of the Box*. n.p.: Elijah List, 2006. Book on-line. Available from http://www.elijahlist.com/words/display_word_pf.html?ID=4189; Internet.

———. "New Apostolic Reformation," Apologetics Coordination Team. http://www.deceptioninthechurch.com.

Foxe. *Foxe's Book of Martyrs*, http://www.ccel.org/ccel/foxe/martyrs/files/fox116.htm.

Good, Chris. "Criticism: Do Not Touch the Lord's Anointed," unknown date. RBC. http://www.rbc.org/nz/library/anointed.htm.

Grady, J. Lee. "Fire in My Bones," Friday, July 27, 2007. Charisma +Online. http://www.charismamag.com/fireinmybones/Columns/show.php.

———. "The Deadly Virus of Celebrity Christianity." *Charisma*, July 2007 [magazine on-line]; available from http://http://www.charismamag.com/fireinmybones/Columns/show.php; Internet.

Hackman, Don. *The Evangelist*. n.p., n.d.

Hamon, Bill. *National School of the Prophets—Mobilixing the Prophetic Office*. Session 11; 5/11/2000.

Hanegraaff, Hank. *Counterfeit Revival*. Nashville: Word Pub., 2001.

———. *Christianity in Crisis*. Eugene, Or.: Harvest House, 1997.

Henry's, Matthew. *A Commentary on the Holy Bible*. 6 vols. Edinburgh: Marshall brothers, limited, 1925.

Hickey, Marilyn. "Widow's Mite Partner Letter." unknown publication date [journal on-line]; available from http://www.Bible.ca/tongues-photogallery-pentecostal-trinkets.htm; Internet; accessed 6 July 2007.

Hinckel, John. n.p., n.d.

"Hindu Gurus and Pentecostal Preachers are Identical," http://www.Bible.ca/tonuge-kundalini-shakers-Charismatics.htm.

Hinn, Benny. *The Anointing*. Nashville, TN: T. Nelson Publishers, 1997.

———. "Benny Hinn: Apologetics Research Resources," Apologetics Index. http://www.apologeticsindex.or/h01ad.html.

———. *Honolulu Blaisdale Crusade*. Hawaii, 1999.

Bibliography

———. TBN *"Praise The Lord."* n.p., 12/30/2002.
———. *Praise-a-Thon* on TBN. n.p., 11/6/1990.
———. "Tape # A031190-1." In *Our Position in Christ*.
Humbard, Rex. "Partner Letter." (1983).
Hunter, Rev. Bradford. "Comparison of God-centered and Man-centered Worship," unknown date. Bradford Hunter. http://www.angelfire.com/nt/theology/godwork2.html.
Jacobs, Cindy. "National School of the Prophets—Mobilizing the Prophetic Office," 2002. http://www.deceptioninthechurch.com/allfalseApostles.html.
Jones, Bob. 1983.
Kaiser, Walter C., Jr. *The Uses of the Old Testament in the New*. Chicago: Moody Press, 1985.
Lloyd-Jones, D. Martyn. *God's Way of Reconciliation: Studies in Ephesians, Chapter 2*. Grand Rapids, Mich.: Baker Books, 1997.
Luther Martin. *ThesIs # 37*. October 31, 1517.
MacArthur, John F., Jr. *Charismatic Chaos*. Grand Rapids, Mich.: Zondervan Pub. House, 1992.
Menzies, William, and Ph.D. *Anointed to Serve*. n.p.: Gospel Publishing House, 1971.
Meyer, Joyce during Interview on *Bible Answer Man*. "Joyce Meyer," Let Us Reason. http://letusreason.org/Popteach17.htm.
Munroe, Myles. *This Is Your Day Broadcast*. n.p.: Benny Hinn Ministries, Inc., 7/13/2004.
Napier, K. B. "The Kansas City Prophets." Bible Theology Ministries. http://www.christiandoctrine.net/doctrine/articles/article_00093_the_kansas_city_Prophets_web.htm.
"The New Violence of the Holy Spirit?," http://www.letusreason.org/Pent33.htm.
Nichols, Stephen J. *Martin Luther's Ninety-five Ttheses*. Phillipsburg, N.J.: P & R Pub., 2002.
Osteen, Joel. Letter from his ministry 2005. Joel Osteen. http://www.myfortresslorg/JoelOsteen.html.
Oppenheimer, Mike. "Apostles and Prophets," Let Us Reason Ministries. http://www.letusreason.org/Pent1.html.
———. "Apostles and Prophets," Let Us Reason Ministries. http://www.letusreason.org/Pent33.html.
Packer, J. I. and O. R. Johnston, Martin Luther's *On the Bondage of the Will*. A new translation of *De servo arbitrio* (1525) Martin Luther's reply to Erasmus of Rotterdam (Westwood, NJ: Revell, 1957).
Pinnock, Clark, and et al. *The Openness of God: A Biblical Challenge to the Traditional Understanding of God*. Downers Grove, Ill.: InterVarsity Press, 1994.
Plass, Ewald M., and comp. *What Luther Says, an Anthology*. Saint Louis: Concordia Pub. House, 1959.
Prasch, Jacob. *Slain in the Spirit: A Midrashic Perspective*. 1996, n.p.
Popoff, Peter. "Prayer Partner Letter." (December 1997).
Reuters. "Pentecostals Buckle up Africa's Bible belt." *Jamaica Gleaner* June 2007 [journal on-line]; available from http://www.jamaica-gleaner.com:80/gleaner/20070630/(spirit)/(spirit)1.html; Internet.
Roberts, Oral. *A Daily Guide to Miracles*. Tulsa: Pinoak Publications, 1978.
———. "Partner Letter Christmas 1982." (1982).
———. *Point of Contact*. Nashville, Tennessee: Thomas Nelson Publishers, 2006.

Bibliography

Roberts, Oral Edition. *Holy Bible.* "My Personal Commentary."

Robertson, O. Palmer. *The Final Word: A Biblical Response to the Case for Tongues and Prophecy Today.* Carlisle, PA: Banner of Truth Trust, 1993.

Sanders, John. *The God Who Risks: A Theology of Divine Providence*, 2d ed. , rev. ed. Downers Grove, Ill.: IVP Academic, 2007.

Schaff, Phillip. "Preface to the Third Edition." In *History of the Christian Church*, Third edition rev. 8 Volumes. Peabody, Massachusetts: Hendrickson Publishers, 7/1/2006. Book on-line. Available from http://http://www.ccel.org/s/schaff/history/About.htm; Internet.

Scrooby, Nicolette. "TBN Seeks Legal Advice on Returning Ill Man's Donation," July 19, 2007. http://www.dispatch.co.za.

Servant, David. "Silver and Gold Have I Quite a Large Sum," June, 2006. Crossbearer.net. http://www.members.tripod.com/crossbearer-brian/id277.htm.

Simpson, Sandy. "Deception in the Church," http://www.deceptioninthechurch.com/New Apostolic Reformationfalsprophecies.html.

———. "False Prophets," http://www.deceptioninthechurch.com/allfalseApostles.html.

———. *New Apostolic Reformation: What Is It and Where Is It going?* n.p.: Apologetics Coordination Team, n.d.

Sproul, R.C. *Chosen by God.* Wheaton, Ill.: Tyndale House Publishers, 1986.

Spurgeon, C. H. *Spurgeon's Sermons.* Volume 5. Grand Rapids: Baker Books, 1999.

Sumerall, Lester. n.p., n.d.

United Pentecostal Church International. "About Us," United Pentecostal Church International. http://www.upci.org/about.asp#oneness.

"United States Geological Society," http://earthquake.usgs.gov/eqcenter/eqarchives/significant/sig_1993.php.

unknown. "Endtime Revival—Spirit-Led and Spirit-Controlled," 2000. *Enrichment Journal* Assemblies of God. http://enrichmentjournal.ag.org/200102/088_endtime_revival.cfm.

Unknown. "Favorite PASTimes: Why Do History—and Historical Fiction—Matter?" http://www.favoritepastimes.blogspot.com/2006/07/why-do-history-and-historical.html.

unknown. "The Potter's House of Dallas—Belief Statement," unknown. Potter's House. http://www.thepottershouse.org/v2/content/view/18/32/.

Van Impe, Jack. n.p., 7/1/1997.

Wagner, C. Peter. *Breaking Strongholds in Your City: How to Use Spiritual Mapping to Make Your Prayers More Strategic, Effective, and Targeted.* Ventura, Calif.: Regal Books, 1993.

———. "Mobilizing the Prophetic Office." *National School of the Prophets*, Session 1 (Friday, 5/12/00, 7pm).

———. "National School of the Prophets—Mobilizing the Prophetic Office," May 11, 2002. http://www.deceptioninthechurch.com/allfalseApostles.html.

———. "National Apostolic-Prophetic Conference." February 2000 [journal on-line]; available from http://www.members.ozemail.com.au/~rseaborn/Apostles.html; Internet; accessed 17 July 2007.

Warfield, Benjamin B. *Counterfeit Miracles.* New York: C. Scribner's, 1918.

Warren, Rick. *The Purpose-driven Life.* Grand Rapids, Michigan: Zondervan, 2002.

Wenthe, Dean O., and M.Div M.A. "Introduction—The Creeds," Concordia Theological Seminary. http://www.ctsfw.edu/academics/faculty/wenthe/creeds.htm.

Bibliography

White, James R. "God-Breathed; Breathed Out By God; Theopneustos," 01/03/2006. Alpha & Omega Ministries. http://www.aomin.org/index.pho?itemid+1193&catid=18.

Wimber, John. *Spiritual Phenomena: Slain in the Spirit*. n.p.: International Association of Vineyard Church, 1981.

Van Impe, Jack. quoting from "On the Edge of Eternity," Religious Tolerance.org. http://www.religioustolerance.org/end_wrl11.htm.

www.ingramcontent.com/pod-product-compliance
Lightning Source LLC
Chambersburg PA
CBHW050802160426
43192CB00010B/1617